Contents

Acknowledgements

The authors would like to thank all those companies and organisations who have talked to us and have given us information for use in this book.

We would particularly like to thank The Training Agency and The Equal Opportunities Commission for making available their research material and Joanna Foster, Chair of The Equal Opportunities Commission for the generous introduction she has written.

We should also like to thank the following people for their generosity in allowing us to publish their research:

David Clutterbuck – Chairman, The ITEM Group for the Beck-Feldmeir Experiment

Ginger Irvine – founder and first president Focus Information Service

Jean Fraser – Corporate Vice-President, American Express, U.S.

Jeanette Taudin-Chabot

For permission to use material delivered at the EFWMD Conference, Brighton 1987

Dr Robin G. Lambert for allowing us to reprint his letter to The Times and for his subsequent correspondence

Dr Susan Winnicombe for her paper on the differences between female and male management styles.

Introduction

This book is part of a challenge – the challenge which faces employers in the 1990s as skills shortages increase; the number of young people entering the labour force decreases; markets widen as national trade barriers are removed; competition becomes fiercer; and workers increasingly expect that a worthwhile career need not mean sacrificing the quality of life, and the quality of family life in particular.

All challenges present opportunities however, and part of this challenge is about making the best use of our human resources; and part of the competition is about finding and hanging on to the 'best people', people who are qualified, multi-skilled, adaptable and highly motivated. In order to compete for these skilled employees, employers are already having to adapt their traditional attitudes and working practices. They are having to sell their organisations; organisations which they hope are seen to be progressive and attractive to their hoped-for recruits. In particular they are having to sell to women. They are having to develop more 'family and women friendly' policies and programmes.

The potential to grow the existing skills and to tap the existing resources of women already within organisations is enormous. So too is the potential to attract young women into non-traditional jobs. Perhaps the most significant area of all this is the need to attract back into the workforce the women who left employment for family reasons and who would now like, and increasingly need, for economic reasons, to return to work. In the UK for instance there is an estimated pool of five million 'economically un-active' women over 25. Women in the UK are taking shorter 'baby breaks' and the fastest rising group of workers is made up of women with pre-school children.

As we know through working with the members of our Equality Exchange and other leading Private and Public Sector organisations many enlightened employers are now taking action to develop different forms of effective equal opportunities policies and practices – Littlewoods, British Rail, Lloyds Bank, the Midland Bank, the National Westminster Bank, Rank Xerox, Thames TV, the BBC, British Telecom, Mars, Esso, British Gas, BP, Royal Insurance are among the leading players – and women will increasingly examine the equal opportunities programmes and reputations of potential employers when considering job offers. What do employers need to do then to develop equal opportunities policies which will attract in, develop and retain women's skills? *Beyond the Great Divide* will tell you!

The major challenge, and opportunity, of the 1990s is for employers to make the maximum use of all the talents available, and for far too long women have been a neglected resource. Employers need the skills of women, and this book shows them how they can become 'women friendly' and attract and retain this valuable source of talent. Women are keen to make their contribution to the changing 90s, their potential is undeniable.

Making equal opportunities a reality is about good Management Practice, managing change and investing in the future. I wish you well in this process.

Joanna Foster
Chair – Equal Opportunities Commission

Preface

This book looks forward to the time when the differences between women and men, young and old, black and white will become meaningless in the context of organisational development.

In 1975 when the Sex Discrimination Act became law, attention was focused on two kinds of discrimination – direct and indirect and it is the latter which is most difficult to define and defeat. Women are capable of indirectly discriminating against other women and men against men. Judgements made by either sex about the other are often based on long standing prejudice and bear no relation to reality.

In the following chapters we shall look at the historical factors which made equal opportunities legislation necessary. The practical application of genuine equality of opportunity is also addressed and a step-by-step approach is used as a guide to achieving it.

The writers have talked to many organisations and give examples of good and inferior practice. The whole spectrum of employment is included from recruitment, through training and development to appraisal and promotion and retention of skills. We have looked in detail at the part played by mentors and at the benefits of networking. The qualities possessed by both women and men have also been examined. These qualities, although different, can be used in tandem to the benefit of any organisation. Finally we look to the future and the skills which will be required by organisations: The changing patterns of work and the roles of corporate wife and husband.

It is our firm belief that every human being irrespective of age, sex or colour has a reservoir of talent which is waiting to be tapped. This talent is composed of knowledge, skill and experience which can blossom and grow or wither and perish depending on the treatment it receives. This statement is no idle dream but is supported by facts and by various scientific studies.

We look forward to the closing of the great divide to the mutual benefit of industry and its personnel.

1 What Is The Great Divide?

The perpetuation of divisions has become a way of life which has been unquestioned in Western society for generations. The UK class system is a perfect example of a division which many would like to sweep away. Others, most notably the public schools, have a vested interest in its survival and so it continues in spite of the strenuous efforts of social reformers, political parties and the more vociferous trade union members.

It seems natural, therefore, that organisations should carry on what has begun in the education system and many companies are characterised by a wide range of divisions such as:

Management versus worker.
White-collar worker versus blue-collar workers.
Black versus white.
Full-time versus part-time.
Oxbridge versus Redbrick.
Heterosexual versus homosexual.
Women versus men.

These differences are characterised by entrenched images which have been accepted without question as in 'working class' – a trade union member wearing overalls, a flat cap and voting Socialist, and 'upper class' – recognisable from smart suit, furled umbrella, rolled up *Times*, an Oxbridge accent and voting Tory.

These are caricatures and will rightly be dismissed as archaic by any right-thinking individual. Other differences are harder to dispel and sweeping judgements are made about individuals simply from the way they look. This is dangerous, particularly during recruitment, when talent and appropriate skill can be dismissed by the interviewer simply because he or she does not like the total package.

The greatest divide of all, and one which has been perpetuated for

Table 1 Percentage distribution of persons in employment by occupational grouping and sex, 1987

Great Britain

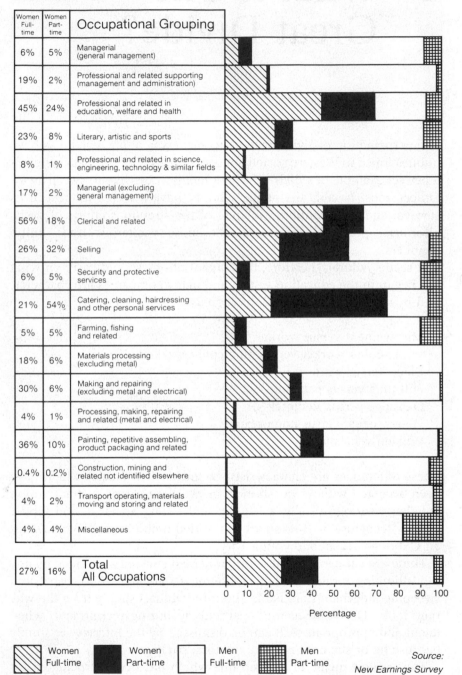

Women Full-time	Women Part-time	Occupational Grouping
6%	5%	Managerial (general management)
19%	2%	Professional and related supporting (management and administration)
45%	24%	Professional and related in education, welfare and health
23%	8%	Literary, artistic and sports
8%	1%	Professional and related in science, engineering, technology & similar fields
17%	2%	Managerial (excluding general management)
56%	18%	Clerical and related
26%	32%	Selling
6%	5%	Security and protective services
21%	54%	Catering, cleaning, hairdressing and other personal services
5%	5%	Farming, fishing and related
18%	6%	Materials processing (excluding metal)
30%	6%	Making and repairing (excluding metal and electrical)
4%	1%	Processing, making, repairing and related (metal and electrical)
36%	10%	Painting, repetitive assembling, product packaging and related
0.4%	0.2%	Construction, mining and related not identified elsewhere
4%	2%	Transport operating, materials moving and storing and related
4%	4%	Miscellaneous
27%	16%	Total All Occupations

Percentage

Women Full-time   Women Part-time   Men Full-time   Men Part-time

Source: New Earnings Survey

thousands of years, is still that which exists between women and men. Certain roles have been forced on both sexes throughout eternity. Gender conditioning begins on the day we are born – pink for a girl and blue for a boy. Little girls learn to please; big boys don't cry. The differences are accentuated throughout education when boys are pushed into science and engineering and girls into art and domestic science.

Table 1 shows how the divide is continuing, 13 years after the introduction of Equal Opportunity Legislation. Men are still in the majority in general management with women representing only 11 per cent (six per cent full-time and five per cent part-time). Women fare rather better in education, welfare and health where 45 per cent of the full-time jobs are occupied by women. This sector of employment is generally lower paid than industry and commerce and represents the caring sector of society where women have always been accepted.

The greatest concentration of women however, are still to be found in clerical and related jobs – 56 per cent full-time and 18 per cent part-time and in catering, cleaning, hairdressing and other personal services where 54 per cent of all jobs are occupied by women who work part-time and another 21 per cent by full-time women workers.

The competence of women has always been recognised in times of crisis, particularly during the world wars when they were dragged away from their domestic surroundings and took their place in industry, medicine, and agriculture as well as maintaining essential services. Once the emergencies were over women were put back on the shelf to make room for the returning heroes. They demonstrated their flexibility by reverting to the housewife role without benefit of pre-retirement counselling or redundancy pay.

Organisations have traditionally valued women as part-time workers, secretaries and, most recently, as 'temps' and this trend continues. These are generally low paid, low status jobs, currently with low security as companies tighten their belts and slim their resources. The role of women in organisations has become an extension of their role at home, i.e. caring and supportive and doing much of the real work but having little power. The majority of organisations are still male dominated and their culture is alien to most women who do not understand the structure, do not know how to make use of it to enhance their own position and are largely unaware of the corporate games that are being played. At the end of the working day the woman may be constrained to get home as quickly as possible in order to resume the domestic role which she has temporarily put aside; she therefore misses the informal networking which takes place in the nearest pub or the sports club, if the company is lucky enough to have one. This corporate happy hour is an excellent way of getting to know colleagues and a vital source of information on who is doing what, who is moving to where, who are the chairman's chosen and much, much more.

Women have been organising, motivating and controlling at least since the Middle Ages. The lady of the manor was very much a working supervisor. The brewing, preserving, horticultural and agricultural activity was controlled by her. In today's world she may be responsible for the domestic budget; she is frequently responsible for the transport – husband to the station, children to school; and whether she organises the washing and cleaning or does it herself it is most certainly her domain.

In organisational terms these skills are recognised as managerial but, until Equal Opportunity Legislation entered the statute books, little effort had been made by organisations to exploit these female skills. If we go back in history and look at one of the women who made an impact in spite of the system we will see that their managerial ability is largely informal.

Florence Nightingale is remembered as the 'lady with the lamp' who walked the wards in the Crimea soothing the fevered brows and bringing comfort to the dying troops. In her first post, as superintendant of the 'Establishment for Gentlewomen During Illness' in Harley Street, she had to manage the nurses, assist at operations and had financial control of the coal cellar and the larder. The experience she gained as organiser and manager as well as nurse and diplomat formed the basis for her future responsibilities in the Crimean war.

A military dispatch, rejoicing over the British-led victory in the battle of the Olnea River, also deplored the fact that little preparation had been made for the care of the wounded. There was a shortage of surgeons, no dressers or nurses, not even a supply of linen with which to make bandages. Florence Nightingale was urged to take out nurses, but refused to do so without official sanction and submitted a plan to Sidney Herbert who was then Secretary for War. Although Herbert knew that a women in any position of public responsibility at that time would create military jealousy and opposition; he was also faced with public indignation at the situation in the Crimea. Florence Nightingale was appointed, with the approval of the Cabinet, to select a group of nurses.

Within a week of arriving in the Crimea she had started a laundry and within ten days she had organised three special diet kitchens to prepare food for the chronically ill who could not take the usual hospital food. She set up a money order department to help soldiers who wished to send pay home and handled £71,000 in her first six months. In return she was charged with officiousness and there was considerable jealousy from both the medical and military personnel. To them it was unendurable that a woman, assisted by the government, should have power and the ability to use it. Some officers sulked, others put up obstacles but the organisation continued as Florence Nightingale created order out of chaos.

After her return to England Lord Stanley is quoted as saying 'she has opened a new profession for women, a new sphere of usefulness'. A grateful country started a fund, which reached £40,000 in a year, and in 1859 the first nursing school was started at St. Thomas's Hospital.

The accomplishments of this woman were remarkable. She demonstrated organisational ability, vision, flair and the determination to change what, until then had been a doubtful occupation, into a profession. Like many other women she triumphed during a crisis but had the vision to continue the work when the crisis was over. She was also unique in offering training to other women, an example which is sadly not always followed today. We have a woman Prime Minister yet only twenty women Members of Parliament, the lowest number since the Second World War.

Active discrimination against women still continues in spite of the fact that Equal Opportunities Legislation forced companies to address it. It was assumed until recently that women's earnings were supplementing the main source of income, that women were working for 'pin-money' and were therefore happy to accept a lower rate of pay for the pleasure of having an income of their own. Women were asked at interview: 'What will you do if the children are sick?' but the question was rarely asked of men. Marriage for men was welcomed as a sign of 'normality' bringing with it a desire to put down roots. Marriage for women signified at one time the end of her career, particularly in the teaching and nursing professions. Even if the new bride continued to work it was assumed that before long she would start a family and give up her career to become a full-time wife and mother. Employers who accepted men back into their jobs after a six-year absence fighting in the Second World War had never considered the possibility of accepting women back after maternity leave, however short that may have been. The employment pattern for women was thus based on their genetic function and their sex rather than on their ability, managerial or otherwise. For this reason they were largely excluded from management development programmes and missed out on the promotional gravy train. It was accepted that men might leave to further their careers and pass on the skills learnt in the organisation for the benefit of a competitor but it was widely felt that it was not worth developing women because they might leave to have babies.

Legal Considerations

The Great Divide continued almost unquestioned until equal pay became a legal requirement by companies. However, little was altered until 1975 when the Sex Discrimination Act became law. Although the Equal Pay Act was introduced in 1970, companies were given until December 1975 to implement the recommendations which were:

1. that women and men had the right to equal treatment as regards terms and conditions of employment when they were employed in:

   (a) the same or broadly similar work, or work which, though different, had been given equal value under a job evaluation scheme.

2. It made provision for discrimination between women and men to be removed from collective agreements, wages orders and employers' pay structures.
3. It applied to men as well as women. Where women doing broadly similar work to men were more favourably treated, e.g. they were entitled to longer breaks, the difference had to be removed by December 1975.
4. It covered all full or part-time female and male employees in manufacturing, service and all kinds of commercial activity. It was permitted to pay lower rates to young workers providing that, age for age, there was no discrimination between the sexes.
5. It applied to all pay and conditions of employment, with limited exceptions – mainly arrangements covering maternity leave, age of retirement and pensions, and statutory controls over women's hours of work.

The screams of protest against this Act will echo down the ages and, in 1988, almost thirteen years after its introduction, cases proving pay discrimination are still being brought against employers, e.g.

Hayward *v* Cammell Laird

Bramley v H & J Quick Ltd.

The Hayward v Cammell Laird case is worth recounting in detail because it represents a legal landmark in the long fight for equal pay for work of equal value.

Julie Hayward was first employed as an apprentice cook and, in company with other male apprentices in Cammell Laird she went to college to study the appropriate City and Guilds courses and subsequently passed her examinations with high marks. The male apprentices were re-graded upwards at the end of their City and Guilds courses, whether or not they passed their examination. Julie was not.

She first took her case to the Equal Opportunities Commission in 1983, the Commission however was unable to help her until January 1984 when the Equal Value Amendment was passed. This amendment was forced on the government by the EEC in order to bring our law into line with the rest of the Community.

Julie asked for her job to be compared with that of thermal insulators, painters and engineers, all of whom worked on board ship. The employer argued that Julie was given free lunches, better sick pay and a better holiday entitlement than the men. This they claimed made her total package as good as that given to the men. The EOC argued that a woman had the right to take home as much money as the men. How do you value sick pay if the employee never gets sick? The case was overturned at the Employment Appeal Tribunal, in the high court but upheld by the House of Lords.

The Sex Discrimination Act 1975 highlighted two kinds of sex discrimination – direct and indirect.

Direct Sex Discrimination

This arises where a person treats a woman, on the grounds of her sex, less favourably than a man is treated.

Indirect Sex Discrimination

This consists of treatment which may be described as equal in a formal sense as between the sexes but discriminatory in its effect on one sex. Indirect sex discrimination arises where a person imposes on a woman who is seeking some benefit (e.g. a job) a condition or requirement with which she must comply in order to qualify for, or obtain, the benefit and where the condition or requirement satisfies all of the following criteria:

1. It is applied equally to men and women.
2. It is such that the proportion of women who can comply with it is considerably smaller than the proportion of men who can comply with it.
3. It is to the detriment of the woman in question because she cannot comply with it.
4. It cannot be shown by the person applying it to be justifiable, irrespective of the sex of the person to whom it is applied, e.g. if an employer were to state that a job required the applicant to be 6ft tall, a woman who was refused the job because of her lack of height would be able to claim indirect discrimination since all the criteria (a) to (d) would be satisfied.

Recruitment Bias

The following extracts, taken from HMSO, Equal Opportunities Commission Research Series: *Barriers to Fair Selection*: by David R. Collinson, give an indication of the extent to which discrimination of one kind or another still exists:

'She was very good but there is only one problem, we don't employ women. She had a perfect profile, the right age, engaging personality, not only that, she was a very good looker . . . yes, she was absolutely ideal, just the wrong sex, so we're not interested.'

Stereotyped assumptions about women as 'homemakers' and men as 'breadwinners' are still common among employers and result in women being recruited for low grade, poorly paid jobs and men for better paid careers with prospects.

'The job is boring, tedious and monotonous. Men wouldn't do it. Women will. It's their temperament. They won't complain, they just get on and do it. It's not a career it's just a job.'

This is a typical comment made by a manager to explain why he only employed women for mundane jobs.

This research shows that informality is often the root cause of sex discrimination. Many companies still do not operate formalised selection procedures or train staff and monitor the consequences. Informality often leads to inconsistent, secretive and unaccountable recruitment practices through which sex discrimination might occur. Selectors still hold stereotyped assumptions which flourish through informal recruitment and promotion procedures. One manager said: 'If the husband doesn't come first he should. . . . The difference for a man is, it is his first commitment to provide for all the family.'

The EOC's code of Practice recommends that informal practices should be avoided and that all employees should be trained in the provisions of the sex equality laws. The sex discriminatory practices of staff are the responsibility of the employer. Companies should also monitor their practices and workforce profile to identify how often and where barriers to equal opportunities are occurring.

Employment Patterns

If we look at current employment patterns they will give us an indication of the distribution of work. The following figures are taken from the Labour Force Survey, 1985, published by the Institute of Manpower Studies:

Numbers of employed – male and female
Full-time male – 11 million
Full-time female – 5 million
Part-time male – 881,000
Part-time female – 4,209,000
Self-employed – 11.2 per cent of all employed
Home based (including live-in jobs) – 7 per cent of all employed
Temporary work female – 1,314,000 i.e. 98 per cent of all temporary workers.

One of the most significant shifts has been the increase in the numbers of married women working. In 1921 married women represented only 3.8 per cent of the labour force. By 1981 the percentage level had increased to 25.9 per cent and it is still rising. There are several reasons for this increase. Modern methods of contraception made it possible for women to plan their families with greater accuracy. Economic trends, most notably the increase in house prices and the cost of living, make it necessary for women to supplement the family income. The numbers of children per family has declined from 2.3 to 1.9 following the baby boom of the late sixties. Sixty-two per cent of all women in the UK between the ages of 16 and 59 now work.

Social Influences

The social trends which have influenced the turning of the tide for working women have been threefold. First the rising divorce rate; one in every three marriages now ends in divorce. In addition, some couples opt to remain unmarried and raise their children out of wedlock. This kind of partnership is perhaps less secure for the woman and she is therefore more inclined to keep up her job. The fear of being left to hold the baby following separation or divorce is quite justified as 12 in every 14 single-parent families are now headed by a woman.

The second major trend to influence women's participation in the labour force has been the high rates of unemployment amongst men. Women's earnings may be the main source of income in the household following redundancy and during any period of unemployment. Rapid changes within industry are eroding the traditional concept of 'a job for life' and men are increasingly having to reconsider their own careers at various stages.

Third there is a growing trend towards greater recognition by women of the importance and necessity to develop a career. Apart from the obvious need for financial security and independence, women, like men, are seeking greater fulfilment from work and are less content to settle for just 'a job'. The expansion of training and educational opportunities now in progress will raise expectations even further with more women presenting themselves for employment in areas tradition-ally dominated by men.

Management Imbalance

The latest information to come from the Department of Employment showing the industrial distribution by sex (1987) tells us that although increasing numbers of women are entering the workforce they are still concentrated in relatively few occupations. The largest single sectors are catering, cleaning, hairdressing and other personal services. So, given the fact that more women than ever before are seeking employment, why is their progress into management jobs so slow?

In 1981 a piece of research was carried out by a project team at Ashridge School of Management. The work was sponsored by the Training Division of Manpower Services Commission (now the Train-ing Agency) and looked at barriers to women's career progression in a cross-section of industries, commerce, and the service and public sectors. The research showed three major factors which inhibited the career development prospects for women:

1. Career paths and personnel procedures.
Career paths were designed to fit the life patterns of men and were

geared to a forty-year period of continuous employment. The fact that many women interrupt their careers has a major impact on their long-term career development. Even though some organisations invite women to follow the same career paths as men, a combination of hurdles still present themselves. The need to acquire professional qualifications, for a broad range of experience and for continuous service, make it difficult for all but the most dedicated to reach the top. Men, on the other hand, are carried along and supported by these factors which create barriers to women.

2. The organisational climate.

There is a general lack of awareness within organisations of the role that women are capable of playing. Senior executives often assume a protective role towards women – the 'don't worry your pretty little head about that' syndrome. Incorrect assumptions are made about the real interests and abilities of women and the types of work to which they are most suited. The most *suitable* jobs for women in this climate include those that require the meticulous application of a detailed body of knowledge, highly specialised jobs and those involving client contact. Women therefore tend to be excluded from the *mainstream* career path and good job performance in a specific area leads to the woman being kept there, rather than promoted, and therefore not developed for wider responsibilities.

3. Women's attitudes and behaviour.

Many women appear to have less confidence in the way they tackle their jobs than their similarly qualified, male colleagues. When describing their strengths and weaknesses women frequently begin by talking about their weaknesses and are diffident about mentioning their strengths. Women can therefore be perceived as 'not wanting to get on'. Men actively try to create conditions for their career advancement; women, on the other hand, tend to sit back and wait to be recognised and rewarded.

Equal Opportunities Policy moves

With the introduction of Equal Opportunity Legislation some companies and several external organisations began to look at the Great Divide and a number of initiatives were set up to deliberately favour women.

Some of these initiatives will be looked at in greater depth later in this book. They can, however, be divided into a few broad categories.

1. Establishing a company profile

This was a data collection exercise and companies looked in detail at several factors:

(a) Numbers of women employed in each grade and/or job category.

(b) Numbers of women responding both internally and externally to advertisements for predominantly male jobs.

(c) Numbers and type of management jobs held by women.

(d) Comparisons of academic and professional qualifications held by women and men.

(e) Age distribution by grade of women and men.

(f) Comparisons of length of service of selected categories of women and men staff, e.g. graduates, professionally qualified staff, supervisory grades.

(g) Comparisons in labour turnover for women and men by grade.

(h) Numbers of women taking maternity leave and those leaving for family reasons.

(i) Analysis of career progression patterns and training records for selected groups of women and men with comparable initial qualifications.

(j) Comparisons of numbers of women and men enrolled in further education for vocational or professional qualifications.

2. Removing recruitment inhibitors.

(a) The use of objective criteria for recruitment and viewing the qualifications for the job rather than the sex of the applicant.

(b) Positive discrimination in favour of women by recruiting them into jobs from which future managers are developed.

(c) Recruitment of women to senior positions.

(d) A statement to the effect that the company viewed itself as an Equal Opportunity Employer.

3 Using objective selection processes

(a) Making sure that a reasonable number of women were included in job interviews.

(b) Using measurable standards to judge the applicant.

(c) Raising awareness of selectors and warning about selecting male stereotypes.

(d) Checking that selection tests, if used, were reliable and valid for women's performance in the job.

(e) Reducing stress of interview by not asking women questions which would not normally be put to men.

4. Equalising reward packages

In the late 1970s, women with comparable qualifications to men appeared by mid-career to earn less. The earnings of a 40-year-old woman was often similar to that of a 30–35-year-old man.

(a) Female and male terms and conditions of employment were examined and differences rectified.

(b) Women and men in comparable jobs were equally graded.

(c) Differences in earnings and benefits were rectified for women and men in comparable jobs.

(d) Part-time workers were paid the same on a pro-rata basis as full-time workers in the same job category.

(e) Differences in pay due to length of service were adjusted.

(f) Part-time workers were included in career development programmes.

(g) Pension provision was equalised.

5. Including women in training programmes

In practice many in-company management development programmes were male dominated. The Sex Discrimination Act allowed companies and other training organisations to discriminate positively in favour of women. This had several beneficial effects:

(a) Some forward-looking companies began looking at the numbers of women and men on management development programmes and made positives efforts to recruit more women in order to equalise the numbers

(b) Other companies ran women-only courses to tackle subjects like long-term career planning and confidence building. Assertiveness training was introduced and has now taken off in a big way.

(c) Some companies instituted accelerated management development programmes for women to enable them to catch up with their male counterparts.

(d) Outside agencies began to initiate training schemes in order to give a boost to women's careers. The majority were funded by the Training Agency. Some operated via the training boards, e.g.

Food, Drink and Tobacco
Hotel and Catering

Chemical and Allied Products
Paper, Printing and Publishing

Others were instituted by management colleges. The Pepperell Unit of
the Industrial Society and local authorities, particularly the GLC and
other London Boroughs.

(a) Attempts were made to run courses which were (a) cheap and (b)
run at a time when women with young families could participate. The
best known of these were the courses run on Saturdays which were
sponsored and marketed through *Cosmopolitan* magazine and run by
the Pepperell Unit.

(b) WOW (Wider Opportunities for Women) and WIM (Women in
Management) courses made their appearance. These were TA funded
and operated via colleges, local authorities and independent providers.

All these initiatives had the collective effect of raising the awareness of
both companies, and the women themselves, of their career potential.
Some of these excellent initiatives will be studied in depth later in this
book. The first attempts to bridge the Great Divide have begun. In the
following pages we shall give advice on the closing of the Great Divide.
It is no longer acceptable to say 'We are an Equal Opportunities
Employer' if promotion is limited to men only.

It would be foolish, however, to put forward a one-sided argument.
The key word is *flexibility* and if companies are becoming more flexible
then the employee will be required to become equally flexible. This may
mean working flat out when demand is high followed by a rest period
when the pace slackens. If women require flexibility for family reasons it
is reasonable in a world geared to equality, for men to require a similar
flexibility. There are already some men who are opting for 'quality of
life', more time with the family and a shorter working week. It should be
easier to satisfy both the needs of the employee and the employer in a
flexi-firm than in the more traditional company geared to 40 unbroken
years of devoted service.

2 Why Bother With An Equal Opportunities Programme?

If we asked you the question 'would you continue to work for a company that didn't offer you the opportunity to develop your career' the majority of you would answer with a very definite 'no'. It is a fact, however, that many managers in companies throughout the UK are oblivious to the talent which is within their grasp and simply waiting to be developed. We include part-time, temporary workers, secretaries and those doing boring and repetitive jobs. Automatic assumptions are made that workers who fall into these categories are 'only working for the money' and 'are not interested in a career'. National research and the opinions we have collected from the many women and men who have attended our courses prove that money frequently comes second to job satisfaction. Few employers addressed the question of equal opportunities before the introduction of legislation. When the Equal Pay Act was introduced in 1970, to be phased in and enforced with the Sex Discrimination Act by 1975, many entrenched employers resented the State's interference, seeing it as a threat to their liberty and profitability. Edwardian values were prevalent at the time with unabashed statements like: 'I see you are wearing an engagement ring, we don't want anything like that, we've been caught before by you young women' (Bradford employer, 1971). This was witnessed at an interview for a secretarial assistant, where women should have expected some consideration, whereas in other jobs, those usually held by men, bald statement like: 'we don't employ women for this job' were quite legitimate and precluded even an application form or an interview.

Although many were sceptical about the ability of the law to change attitudes it did force employers to take heed of such overt discrimination. The traditional employer was loathe to be seen to be operating outside the law and the penalties could be time-consuming and expensive. Some loopholes, such as renaming jobs, were often found to compensate for the inconvenience. The law forced employers to reconsider their position regarding the employment of women and continues to be a prime reason for positive action in favour of women.

Proposed Equal Treatment Act

The amount of legislation controlling sex discrimination is likely to be increased if proposals made by the Equal Opportunities Commission and the EEC for a new Equal Treatment Act are accepted. Several amendments are proposed with the aim of narrowing exceptions and simplifying existing provisions. For example, the EOC call for the expansion and clarification of the indirect discrimination provisions. Two measures would allow this:

(a) making any practice that has an adverse effect on one sex open to challenge (thus avoiding the problem of strictly defining a 'requirement or condition'); and

(b) adopting as the test of 'justifiability' that adopted by the European Court of Justice (where discriminatory provision is justified if there are genuine economic reasons for its existence).

The European Parliament is presently considering the De Backer Van Ocken report which finds that indirect discrimination of women still exists in the application and adoption of the EEC equal treatment directives into national legislations. The report also urges the Commission to come up with a precise definition of indirect discrimination.

It is also proposed that the remaining exceptions relating to 'death or retirement' in both the Equal Pay Act and the Sex Discrimination Act be repealed. The Commission clearly reassert their long-standing recommendation that the pension age be equalised as soon as possible, recognising that a reasonable transition period would be necessary to implement the change. Also in the employment field, the EOC proposes several changes to the 'genuine occupational qualification' defence open to employers, a tightening-up of the way the law applies to clients of recruitment agencies, and a strengthening of the 'victimisation' provisions, including increased compensation. A radical shift in the 'burden of proof' is also seen as crucial so that unaided applicants are not deterred from claiming. The Commission propose that, once an applicant has proved less favourable treatment in circumstances consistent with grounds of sex, family status or victimisation, a presumption of discrimination should arise which would then have to be rebuffed by the respondent.

Pregnancy and family policy

The EOC point out that the increased use of the Sex Discrimination Act to challenge pregnancy dismissals has severe limitations. There can be problems in identifying a comparator, and if an employer can show that he would have treated a man equally badly, a woman would have no claim. Instead they propose that the most effective protection for women would be to abolish the two-year qualification period for the 'right to return' and for challenging pregnancy dismissals. In the longer term, they say that separate legislation for maternity rights may be necessary. The European Committee for Women's Rights has called upon the European Commission, to draw up a proposal, applicable in all EEC countries, which will provide certain facilities for pregnant women before, during and after the birth.

The new, comprehensive Equal Treatment Act would cover sex discrimination by reference to both 'marital' and 'family' status – concepts expressly included in European Community Law. The EOC believes that issues such as child-care facilities and the tax implications of child care expenses and parental leave, cannot be dealt with through equal treatment legislation alone. The Commission therefore calls for a family policy to complement the new legislation on equal treatment.

Local Authorities

Another change would be the introduction of a duty on public bodies to work towards eliminating discrimination and promoting equal opportunity between women and men. This would influence the provision of services, for example to support carers, which meet the needs of women and their families. It would also bring the Equal Treatment Act into line with the Race Relations Act and have a knock-on effect on contract compliance in the Local Government Bill. The new EEC directive on public procurement contains a separate declaration calling on all contractors to observe statutory regulations on equal opportunities.

Enforcement

The Commission made several proposals aimed at strengthening their powers of formal investigation (at the same time reducing the burden on individuals), as well as expediting the procedure in these investigations – although they recognise that such proposals will not be universally popular. As far as individual proceedings are concerned, the EOC again propose that specialised training be given to all tribunal and Employment Appeal Tribunal members, that efforts continue to be made to increase the number of women members, and that a woman is included in the panel in all equal treatment cases.

In 'Legislating for Change?' the Commission asked for views on whether there should be minimum levels of compensation, and they now propose that in successful discrimination claims there should be a basic minimum award of £500 or four weeks' pay (whichever is the higher), in addition to any award for injury to feelings. They also call for compensation to be payable in cases of indirect discrimination whether or not the discrimination was intentional. In addition, it is proposed that all awards should attract interest until paid and should be enforceable directly in the county courts.

Balancing pay

Traditionally women have been employed as cheap labour; however, the Equal Pay Act 1970 was designed to remove discrimination between men and women in pay and other conditions of their contract of employment. Yet despite 20 years of its operation women's earnings remain only 73 per cent of men's gross hourly rates. This is usually because their jobs are graded at lower levels to comply with the law. This is relatively simple to do where large numbers of women work in specialised areas like checkout operators, secretaries, cleaners and canteen assistants. Job evaluation schemes often carry an inbuilt bias against women by failing to place value on skills such as caring or dexterity. The anomalies caused by a strict comparison between 'jobs of a broadly similar nature' led to the 1983 Equal Value Regulations which applied the principle of equal pay for work of equal value. The Regulations were soon tested in 1984 by Miss Hayward of Cammell Laird as described in detail in the previous chapter. In her case an independent expert was employed to make comparisons between the various jobs in terms of physical and environmental demands, decision making, skill, knowledge and responsibility. These were each graded in broad terms as either low, moderate or high. The precedent set by Miss Hayward's case has given cause for employers universally to re-examine their job evaluation schemes and the criteria to be used for grading. Not only has it become illegal to overtly discriminate against women but it is now less possible to rationalise lower pay without just cause.

The judgement made in the Hayward *v.* Cammell Laird case has two major implications for employers: first it is no longer necessarily cheaper to employ a woman than a man and secondly that women do have special skills and experience to contribute to an organisation which can be measured by a proper job evaluation scheme.

The constant effect of downgrading women's skills has been to reinforce their own perceptions of inadequacy rather than to encourage or motivate women to develop and contribute more effectively to the organisation. If pay is equated with status and performance then raising the levels of women's pay or providing greater opportunity to earn more pay, is likely to increase women's sense of responsibility towards the company.

The employers who are likely to gain are those who recognise that the employment of cheap labour is merely a short-term gain, in the long term the company benefits more by recognising and cultivating the skills and experience of their employees and then by being able to retain them.

A survey sponsored jointly by Brook Street Bureau and *Elle* magazine, was carried out in June 1988. The survey was designed to explore the attitude women had to their work. The *Elle* readership is young, 18–25, and the socio-economic grouping high, AB1. More than half the respondents were educated to degree level or higher. Most were single, but two in every five respondents were married or living with a partner. Forty-eight per cent of the respondents were professional women and a third held management positions. In spite of this, almost half earned less than £10,000. Only one in five respondents earned more than £15,000. If the following findings are true for this group of women who are articulate and, presumably, aware of their legal rights, what is working life like for those with fewer qualifications. Sixty per cent of the women said they were expected to do things at work that men were not; this rose to 72 per cent when looking solely at clerical staff. A marketing and research executive told how she was passed over for promotion in order that a man moving to her department could take the job. He had less experience and fewer qualifications. Nine months later he was moved on and she was given the job, initially on a three months trial. Her pay rose from £8,000 to £8,800 when she was finally given the job on a permanent basis. Her predecessor had been earning £15,000 and a male colleague with similar responsibilities earned £17,000. When she told her employers she felt she was worth more they said they felt they had been fair – by paying her slightly more than half the considered wage for a man!

In spite of this and many other similar examples of blatant discrimination against women, the majority of the respondents wanted to work. Only 8 per cent said they would like to stop altogether and 63 per cent said they would work even if they did not need the money.

Job satisfaction and a sense of achievement were cited as the main motivators for women at the top end of the spectrum. They also enjoyed the power, responsibility and authority; the feeling of doing a worthwhile job and of being needed. In contrast, women in manual or clerical work short on job satisfaction put money before anything else, followed by partners and then friends. Work for its own sake was their fourth priority which is hardly surprising given the nature of their jobs.

Balancing status

It would appear therefore that, although it has become fashionable for many companies to have an equal opportunities policy the statements made therein do not always filter through to the workers for whom it was intended. It seems that in many cases, the document amounts to little more than an acknowledgement of the legal constraints imposed by the Act.

An equal opportunities policy statement is useless on its own whether hidden in the filing cabinet or displayed in the staff manual. It needs rather to be imprinted on the minds and interpreted in the practices of all those employed by the company. As a written statement only it does little to counteract the most common type of sex discrimination that occurs nowadays. This follows the indirect format through traditional practices which operate to the disadvantage of women. Recruitment through the grapevine or age limitations which put female returners at a disadvantage are still widely practised in spite of the legislation.

The subtle form in which this type of discrimination takes place may mean that it happens without the full realisation of many employers. Yet in practice it inhibits a major source of employee development, creating blocks to the skills and management potential within the organisation. Amongst the many thousands of secretaries, clerks, assistants and line operators employed there are many who have the potential to become successfully trained as technicians, computer operators, supervisors or managers. Overlooking this factor creates a high cost for both companies and employees. Many of these employees have already developed a high level of competence and experience. If this is frustrated by lack of opportunity, employee potential will be lost to the employer because of frequent job changing. If and when a woman ceases work to have a family she will not be encouraged to return to an employer who offers no career progression. Most employers are aware of the high cost of recruitment and induction training due to staff turnover so it makes sense to give incentives for employees to stay.

Economic balance

The argument for having an equal opportunities policy that works is as much an economic one as a social one. This is increasingly so with the changes currently taking place in the labour market. Many industries are already beginning to experience problems in recruiting labour notably banks, hotels, nursing and service industries in general. This shortfall is likely to extend across the board with the number of school-leavers expected to decline by one third in 1992 and the demand for skilled labour continuing to grow. Companies in areas of work traditionally chosen by men, such as engineering, are beginning to realise a shortfall of new entrants which cannot be satisfied by traditional recruitment sources. At the same time that employers are seeking to increase and upgrade their workforce there is a parallel train in female participation in the workforce with more women wanting to play a greater role in commerce and with corresponding recognition. Employers must therefore realise that it makes economic sense to utilise the skills women have to offer to their fullest. By enabling women to fill in the gaps they can continue to satisfy the manpower needs of both now and the future.

Raising standards

Increasing the pool of labour for economic reasons is not simply a question of finding another source to replace one that can no longer provide the numbers required. To talk in these terms carries a sugges-tion that the pool of female labour has long been overlooked for many occupations because it is second best. There is no logic at all in this view if we look at the success rates of pupils at school. For example, a case of discrimination was brought against the 11+ examining authorities in Ireland for equalising the number of boys and girls passing the exam. In fact, more girls had higher marks than boys and were therefore being downgraded in favour of 'equality'. It may be possible to identify a number of differences in the way boys and girls behave in the playground but in the classroom, where ability is identified, girls can often outshine the boys. It is a reflection on our culture that brainpower and ability becomes redirected at later stages. Women now make up nearly half the working force but rather than having their talents and abilities recognised, they function as a grossly under-used resource. The further up the hierarchy one goes in a company, the less likely one is to meet a woman. One is bound to ask what effect on managerial excellence would occur if women were given the same opportunities for development as men?

Increasing the pool of labour is not so much a question of recruiting more women. It is rather placing those women in a better position to contribute their skills, both technological and managerial, which are so urgently needed for the health and competitiveness of industry both now and in the future. Companies need to look at increasing the pool of talent by offering training and employee development programmes to ensure that each person contributes to their maximum potential. An equal opportunities programme that is concerned with these issues will actively seek to promote excellence in individuals, recognising this as sound commercial sense.

Research carried out by the Training Agency, before the introduction of its first Adult Training Strategy, looked in detail at skill shortages in various parts of the UK. They discovered that employers were much more likely to poach skills from other companies than to develop their own staff to fill the vacancies.

A consistent demotivating factor, which is frequently discussed on the courses which we ourselves run, is that of low self-esteem. The employee frequently feels undervalued by the company for which s/he works. A most frequent reason for leaving organisations is given as 'I just wasn't getting anywhere!'

Raising commitment and motivation

We have already mentioned the possible negative effects of downgrading jobs in terms of pay and status. This is an important point because it relates to the 'labelling theory' which is taught to all trainee teachers. In effect, if a teacher is told in advance that certain pupils are poor achievers, her expectations of their performance will be lowered and they, in turn, will respond in the way they are perceived. Experiments with groups of children have also shown the reverse to be true. If a group of children are treated as bright and co-operative, they will respond better than their counterparts who have been downgraded.

In similar style an experiment was performed in Canada to highlight racial awareness by labelling children in a school class according to their eye colouring. The children with dark eyes were treated as the bad guys on one day and then their roles were reversed on the second day. The results showed how easy it became to believe in the labels and how damaging it felt to those who had been badly labelled, even on a temporary basis. Many of the labels that are attached to women, ethnic minorities or disabled people have been sticky enough to both block their opportunites within an organisation while at the same time lowering their expectations of what they can achieve.

This question of labelling was raised by a correspondent in the *Elle* survey. She had taken a year away from the Bar to think about where her career was going and said:

> I began to lose a sense of myself; there was no convenient way to define myself any more. I would actually miss people saying 'What do you do?' which is almost synonymous with 'what are you?' I don't think of myself as a silly, trivial person who needs a label, but I think my self has merged with what I do.

Those who are uncomfortable with their labels find their self-esteem drops. A teacher said: 'I'm embarrassed now to say I am a teacher because people – or, at least, the press – have a low opinion of teachers in this country. Also it's an unglamorous profession.'

Getting the best out of people is about valuing their contribution and recognising their commitment through pay and promotion. Providing opportunities for employees to develop is one of the best forms of motivation possible and a well planned equal opportunities programme contains all the elements necessary to make this happen. The very fact that an active programe is being introduced will raise expectations by demonstrating interest and care shown by the employer. The inevitable and welcome outcome of an equal opportunity programme is change, and for women it is demonstrably change for the better. Men too come to recognise this – once the repercussions of an active form of employee development takes place in one area it must influence employee development generally.

Improved training

One of the ways in which both men and women benefit from the implementation of an equal opportunities programme is through the training which becomes a necessary part of the process. Programmes generally start with awareness raising sessions in which both men and women take part and then go on to include courses such as interviewing and appraisal techniques to eliminate bias in these areas. The very fact that these training courses are designed to heighten awareness of the problems which may be caused by standard or traditional employment practices makes them more specific about training objectives. More care must be taken in their design to ensure effectiveness. Not only is this likely to raise the standards of training but it may mean that training takes place where it has been overlooked or not considered necessary before. The personnel manager may have undergone this kind of training in the natural course of her/his job but line managers may not although s/he may be called to conduct interviews or staff appraisals on a regular basis.

There may be other forms of training which have never been seriously considered until the introduction of an equal opportunities programme. In particular courses relating to employee development, including career planning workshops, assertiveness training and presentation skills. The value of interpersonal skills training is increasingly being recognised and the introduction of an equal opportunities policy may well provide the impetus to get things going. Although some of the skills are identified as urgently needed by women to catch up with their male counterparts, these courses invariably find great popularity amongst male employees who are just as keen to progress up the career ladder but need some encouragement.

Improving the effectiveness of individuals inevitably leads to an improvement in the effectiveness of the training programmes which are designed to enhance the learning process. The changes brought about in employees attitudes are often quite striking and visible results are shown in the number of promotions which ensue and the desire of some employees to retrain into non-traditional areas of female employ-ment which are opened up as a result of such a programme.

Generally it must be seen that planning and implementing an equal opportunities programme calls for higher training standards to achieve the desired results, i.e. a motivated, skilled and committed workforce. A worthwhile investment for any employer.

Greater flexibility

Many companies are now faced with a constantly changing commercial environment and are therefore seeking greater flexibility within their workforce. A leaner staff combined with technological innovations have caused companies to require employees who can demonstrate greater versatility in their working practices to cope with fluctuations in production and output. The improvement of training facilities and the widening of opportunities brought about by implementing an equal opportunities programme encourage the kind of flexibility necessary to service the business. Those involved in the training programmes will probably gain a broader perspective of the functions contained within the company and are thus more willing to move around the various departments. The added experience this is likely to bring increases their value to the organisation; for example, when a typist is trained to be a supervisor she carries her typing skills with her. One of the main outcomes identified by women who have taken part in an equal opportunities programme is the development of greater confidence. Part of this results from learning to improve the planning and execution of their duties which enables them to exercise greater control over their jobs. This confidence is an essential tool for employees who are asked to exercise greater flexibility. Moving to a different department or taking on new tasks is much less intimidating to those employees who have developed the ability to feel they can master anything new given the right level of support.

Flexibility through equal opportunities also includes looking at more versatile working patterns. These are examined in more detail in Chapter 11. Women are providing an impetus for employers to review the need for all employees to work standard 9–5 hours which have severe limitations for many workers. In doing so they are demonstrating that hours of work can be adjusted to the needs of the organisation as well as the individual.

Complementary management skills

The women's movement have increasingly edged away from trying to compete with men on male grounds. Instead, women are recognising that what experiences and attitudes they have to offer may in some areas be different from men's but nevertheless equally valid and useful. Investigations have shown that there are differences in the operating styles of male and female managers, but that these are in fact complementary rather than contradictory.

Some interesting research into the major differences between female and male managers, was carried out at Cranfield School of Management by Dr Susan Vinnicombe. She used the Myers Briggs Type Indicator (MBTI), which is based on Jung's personality types. This research produced some significant findings on the differences between female and male working styles.

The MBTI aims to gauge, from a self-completed questionnaire, the basic preferences of individuals with respect to perception and judgement. The MBTI contains separate dimensions for determining each of the four basic preferences which, according to Jung, structure the personality of the individual. The four preferences are:

1. Extroversion or introversion

Jung identified two main ways in which people relate to each other, either extrovert or introvert. Extroverts tend to be happier when working with people or things. They have a sociable, talkative, impulsive profile; enjoy a variety of tasks and are stimulated by unanticipated interruptions, Introverts tend to be more interested and contented when their work requires a lot of quiet reflection and thought. They present themselves as quiet, shy individuals who like to concentrate on a few tasks at a time and dislike unanticipated interruptions. No one is totally extrovert or introvert: we can all behave in either way at various times.

2. Sensing or intuition

Gathering information is a key role for a manager. Jung tells us that there are two main ways in which we gather it – in a sensing or an intuitive way. Sensing tells you what is actually happening. Sensing people prefer practical problems, systems and methods, are patient with routine details and look for standard problem-solving approaches. Intuition shows meanings, relationships and possibilities that are beyond the reach of senses. Intuitive people therefore enjoy ambiguous problems, are bored by routine problems, ignore the facts frequently and search for creative approaches.

3. Thinking or feeling

Managers are ultimately assessed on the quality of their decisions rather than how they deal with information or manage their relationships. Decisions are made in two ways. Thinking centres on the logical outcome of a particular action and decisions are made impersonally on the basis of cause and effect. Thinking people try to establish objective decision-making criteria, they are seen as detached, they like clarity and analysis and will negotiate on the information available. Feeling people have subjective decision-making criteria and can be seen as biased. They like harmony based on common values and negotiate on the rights and wrongs of the issue in question.

4. Judgemental and perceptive

We all make choices on how to allocate time priorities. Some people want a lot of information before they make a decision, they are the perceptive types. Others make decisions quickly in spite of the fact that they have little data, they are judgemental individuals. Perceptive people enjoy searching out new information, are tolerant of ambiguity and are concerned to know, not to organise. Judgemental people like clarity and are concerned with resolving issues.

Each of the four dimensions is independent of the other three which gives us sixteen combinations of personality types in all. The MBTI classifies people according to their combination of preferences along the four dimensions, for example an ESTJ indicates a preference for Extroverted, Sensing, Thinking and Judgemental rather than Introversion, Intuition, Feeling and Perception.

These sixteen pure personality types were reduced to five managerial types by the Centre for Creative Leadership in Ohio, USA. These five types were used at Cranfield to compare female and male working styles.

Traditionalists (these all share the preferences for 'sensing' and 'judgemental')

Strengths
    Practicality, common sense
    Seldom make errors of facts
    Good with systems and procedures
    Uphold values of the organisation
    Steady, hard workers
    Super dependable
    Follow through on commitments
    Realistic about time requirements

Weaknesses
    Inclined to decide issues too quickly
    May not be responsive to changing needs of organisation
    May not be good at handling work relationships
    May be overly concerned with possibility of things going wrong

Catalysts (these all share the preferences for 'intuition' and 'feeling')

Strengths
    Personal charisma and commitment to staff

Communicate care and enthusiasm
Excel in working with people
Comfortable in unstructured, complicated situations

Weaknesses
Can be too drawn into pleasing others
Difficulties in carrying out rules and regulations
May spend too much time seeking approval of others
May avoid unpleasantness and difficulties
Tendency to take over other peoples' troubles

Visionary (these all share the preferences for 'intuition' and 'thinking')

Strengths
Intellectual orientation
Creative and progressive
Enjoy solving problems
Excellent decision makers
May be outspoken in their views

Weaknesses
May be insensitive to feelings of others
May devalue colleagues not as intellectual as themselves
Difficulties in handling relationships because they expect so much of people
May feel restless and unfulfilled

Trouble shooter/negotiator (these all share the preferences for 'sensing' and 'perspective')

Strengths
Pragmatists
Don't fight the system, but use what is available to solve problems
Welcome change
Know what is going on in an organisation
Responsive to immediate demands

Weaknesses
Reluctant to deal in the abstract
Can react negatively to extreme change

Adaptable until system is violated

May be seen as unpredictable and unreliable (because they focus on the immediate)

The Cranfield research was carried out in August 1986 using three different groups of women.

1. A group of 25 female students who were completing a 12-month MBA programme at Cranfield. All the students had a minimum of three years work experience. Their backgrounds varied from marketing to computing, finance, personnel, research and development, teaching and the armed forces.
2. Forty-two women belonging to the National Organisation for Women's Management Education (NOWME). These women tend to be in middle or senior positions or they are entrepreneurs. The majority were in some aspect of human resource management (personnel, training, education, counselling).
3. Twenty middle managers from British Telecom attending a Women in Management programme at Cranfield. They were all specialists, many in computing, engineering and finance.

Results

The Myers Briggs results for the three samples of female managers, analysed according to the Centre for Creative Leadership types, are shown in Table 2. There are some differences across the three samples,

Table 2

	Traditionalists	Trouble Shooters/ Negotiators	Catalysts	Visionaries
Cranfield	56.9%	10.7%	10%	22.4%
Female MBA students n=25	24%	4%	32%	40%
NOWME females n=42	28.6%	7.1%	40.5%	28.6%
British Telecom female managers N=20	25%	20%	10%	40%

probably related to the background positions of the female managers. There are significant differences between the three female samples and the norms established by the Centre for Creative Leadership and Cranfield.

The Centre for Creative Leadership did a percentage breakdown of the five types which was almost exactly corroborated by the Cranfield database (849 managers attending short courses – almost exclusively male). These two sets of figures are shown in Figure 1, the shaded

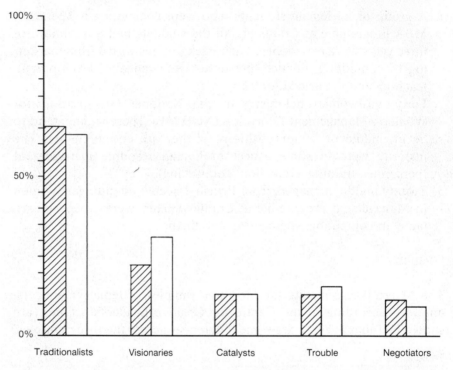

Figure 1 *Breakdown of managerial styles based on the Centre for Creative Leadership at Cranfield*

columns show the Cranfield figures.

The major difference is a marked lack of 'traditionalists' amongst the female managers. A total of 56.9 per cent of male managers tend to be 'traditionalists' compared with an average of 25.9 per cent for the female managers. This finding fits with the common criticisms of women managers as being:

'critical of the organisation'
'too independent'
'poor with systems and routines'
'impractical'

'poor at meeting deadlines'

The women managers did not show an overwhelming preference for a particular management type. Significantly more women managers are 'visionaries' and 'catalysts'. Across all three samples there is a marked increase in the percentage of visionaries compared with male managers (28.6–40 per cent). The majority of female managers from the British Telecom and MBA course were, in fact, 'visionaries'. This is particularly interesting if we look at the few women who achieve senior positions in today's organisation. 'Visionaries' are supposed to be the 'natural' strategic managers.

The percentage of female managers in the NOWME and MBA samples who are 'catalysts' are very much higher than the 10 per cent norm (40.5 per cent and 32 per cent). If one looks at the strengths and weaknesses of the 'traditionalists' – predominantly male group and the 'catalysts' and 'visionaries' – predominantly female except for the British Telecom sample, it is easy to see that the three styles can be complementary. The organisation which actively develops a good mix of management styles will be richer with good creativity, interpersonal and problem-solving skills coupled with the maintainers of organisational values and procedures.

It is not good enough, in today's organisational climate, to value women for their caring and nurturing qualities and their good interpersonal skills. It is for these reasons that women managers have been directed into the personnel and welfare departments. These departments are not normally seen as launching pads for general managers. Work in either can be used as part of the development process for both female and male managers, but not as a final resting place for aspirant women.

An organisation is much more likely to get a good mix of managers by using a more scientific means of selection such as the MBTI. An effective balance can then be obtained which utilises both female and male managerial styles. The training programmes can be aimed to counteract the weakness, e.g. time management skills for women, interpersonal skills for men. Company personnel, at whatever level, are much more inclined to give their loyalty to an organisation which values their skills. By building on strengths and helping to minimise weaknesses the company is demonstrating its ability not only to recruit appropriate talent but to work hard to retain and develop it. It is totally unrealistic to expect anyone to stay in an organisation where they cannot progress.

3 Gaining Commitment

At the 1988 Annual General Meeting of the National Organisation for Women's Management Education, Joanna Foster, Head of the Equal Opportunities Commission, stated: 'We are past the stage of why Equal Opportunities and are now at the stage of how.' The changes for 1992 are already in progress, and we must look to ways of making manpower resources more effective by reassessing the contribution made by women. However, an Equal Opportunities Officer cannot assume that either a statement of policy, or his/her appointment, guarantees the right attitudinal climate for the kind of commitment to equality that will penetrate all levels of the organisation. It is only a starting point for the changing of values and attitudes that have been inherent in our culture over many centuries. For most people it will require a major adjustment of assumptions and beliefs that lie mainly at a subconscious level. The process will involve a re-evaluation of the basis of role conditioning from the cradle onwards.

We need to understand the causes of stereotyping from both an economic and a social context. These stem from two basic premises:

1. Economic. Men are breadwinners therefore should be given priority in training and jobs.
2. Social. Women are carers and nurturers whose priority is homemaking and family rearing thus making them less committed to work and better suited to a supporting role.

Despite all the evidence to the contrary, these assumptions remain the greatest barrier to progress beyond the great divide. It is in these areas that we must start the process of changing attitudes by raising awareness of both men and women through challenging all the prevalent stereotyped assumptions about the roles of men and women. Many of the offending attitudes may be subtle, like assuming when someone refers to an unknown manager that it is a him rather than a her or that women mind making the tea less than men.

Some assumptions are more obvious and damaging like taking for granted that secretarial staff are unlikely to want to seek career progression beyond the role of secretary. This is a particularly interesting example in view of the fact that the first secretaries were male and the secretarial role was part of a planned career. The men in question usually went on to fulfil more senior jobs in the organisation. With the advent of the typewriter women began to move into the secretarial role and the career professional stopped. Promotion for secretaries is linked to the person for whom they work – from typing pool to managing director's personal assistant. This pattern is beginning to change, however, as the shape of organisations change. Secretaries are increasingly seen as playing a pivotal role in a satellite group of managers and their training needs are being examined by some forward looking companies.

One of the problems with all types of assumptions is that they are rarely challenged simply because they underline traditional practice which, having established a pattern over many years, is difficult to break. If a woman has been making the tea ever since she started working in the department it takes a great deal of courage to announce one day she is no longer happy to do this.

Starting from the top

Change on any scale that relates to organisational development must start with total commitment from those who have the power and authority to begin the process. This is essential to guarantee the credibility of the policy as well as the dynamic required to gain commitment. The well publicised and highly acclaimed equal opportunities policy of Littlewoods Stores owes much of its success to the initiative of John Moores, the company's chairman. It was through his concern about the lack of opportunity for women and black workers that a five-year plan for improvement in recruitment and development practices was established. When he set up his equal opportunites unit he made sure that he personally chaired the quarterly meetings of the equal opportunities working group. This policy will be described in detail in the next chapter.

Penetrating the top levels

The committed person from the top must also carry with him/her senior management who are capable of devolving the process. In most companies the group of people in this position have acquired their seniority through long-term career development. Many of these senior executives have attributed part of their success to the fact that they have been supported along the way by a wife who has relieved them of most of the responsibility for running a home and rearing a family. When George Bush was elected for the American presidency it was identified that his wife had been prepared to move 29 times during the course of his career and 17 of these moves were to different cities. Clearly Mrs Bush has made a career of supporting her husband and their five children.

Many of the men at the top have been able to devote their whole time and attention to work, travelling abroad freely, moving location when necessary and being able to come home exhausted to a well-organised household with dinner on the table and clean shirts ready for the next day. It is against this knowledge that a programme of awareness must tackle the issue of changing roles with a recognition that it may take a quantum leap to convince some men that this 'balanced' state of affairs must change.

Commitment from the top may be easy to acquire in terms of the organisation's interests: the advantages of a better trained and higher motivated workforce are obvious, but what if this involves the Managing Director's own wife? What if it means asking him to forfeit the advantages of full-time support and leads to conflict of interest between his working needs and his wife's? Clearly awareness raising at this level will present a challenge which must be met on the basis that if this hurdle can be overcome, it will set the pattern throughout. It will be a testing ground for recognising not just the barriers within personal perceptions but of weighing the balance between individual objectives and corporate objectives. If a manager accepts the need for equal opportunities within the company but not in his own life then change has not been effective. If a man has not been able to develop an inner conviction that it is just as right and necessary for a woman to develop opportunities and seek self-fulfilment through work then he will continue to represent a barrier to real progress.

Working from the positive

Changing attitudes can only work from the positive. If men see women's equality as a threat to their position then any programme is doomed to failure. It is well-tried sales practice to sell the advantages of a product, what will it do for the customer? How will the company benefit from implementing an equality programme? What will the individual manager gain from this process? What benefits are there to men generally from living and working in a less divided world? How can managers be made to recognise the sheer social injustice of treating a woman less favourably than a man? How can managers be convinced that creating opportunities for women will broaden their perspective, bring greater flexibility and choice for all, whether within the organisation or in their personal lives? Being the sole breadwinner may have limitations which far out-weigh the advantages of having slippers warming by the fire. Change and uncertainty can be far more threatening to one's security than having a wife who is developing a career. Redundancy and career changes happen as often to men as to women and a dual career family can be a safeguard against some of the consequences. This is not simply wishful thinking on the part of women in general and some in particular. Between 1982 and 1984 300,000 men left the labour market. In the same period 600,000 new jobs were created, 400,000 of these being created by individuals. But women took 500,000 of the new jobs thus leaving 200,000 men in the dole queue. According to Professor Charles Handy, a specialist adviser to the Commons Select Committee on Employment, only half the population will have full time jobs by the end of the century. The rest will be self-employed, working part-time or unemployed.

Identifying the problem

There are a great many issues to be talked about during the initial phases of the awareness raising process but the starting point must be identifying the problem. Senior managers must be convinced that there is a problem in the utilisation of manpower resources relating to the recruitment and progression of women within the company. There are two levels on which this can operate.

1. Corporate level. This can be identified by monitoring the personnel records to show the numbers of women recruited, their levels of qualification and types of employment, the amount of training given, promotion achieved and the proportion of women reaching higher levels within the organisation. If national trends are reflected in these figures they will clearly show a wide disparity between the positions of men and women.

These facts and figures may be placed alongside facts relating to conditions in the labour market together with forecasts for manpower needs in the future. For example, figures published by the Hotel and

Catering Industry project an average growth rate of 2.5 per cent, requiring 134,000 more employees by 1990, the highest proportion of whom are managers. If this is set against the estimated reduction of 1.2 million school-leavers by 1995 when the workforce is expected to grow by 900,000 in the same period, it is clear that women will constitute an even more important sector of the workforce.

Many other industries are facing similar problems, especially in the service sector, so full weight should be attached to the specific needs of the company through corporate and manpower plans.

2. Departmental level. Awareness raising at this level relates more directly to the individual manager's job. The efficiency of a department rests largely on the development of the skills of its members and retaining the experience that has been accumulated. The loss of any one trained worker presents problems of recruitment, new training and the ability to delegate responsibility. Few managers nowadays have either the time or resources to accept these losses lightly yet they may be quite unaware of the possibility that some losses may be quite unnecessary. It is well known that many secretaries are lost through boredom and lack of challenge, even where they work for men with excessive workloads. The example of just one woman interviewed prior to writing this book serves to illustrate this point. She had developed advanced skills in all aspects of secretarial work but spent years seeking a job that offered her real scope for challenge. Eventually she managed to find a boss in an engineering company who had sufficient confidence in himself and her ability to delegate the level of responsibility she needed to feel truly stretched and develop. Her efforts were recognised and her commitment to her boss and the company were strengthened. This was clearly demonstrated when her company moved location from Yorkshire to the Midlands and she was prepared to move with them for the initial period of settling in, despite the lengthy commuting that was involved. This could only be a temporary measure but, as a result of her experience with the company, she moved on from being a secretary to a new job as a consultant with a company of professional recruitment experts.

Many highly trained women are lost during maternity leave simply because no thought has been given to ways in which they can be given the time necessary to adjust to their new role whilst maintaining links with the job in order to return to work. Faced with the choice between total loss or temporary loss of a valued member of the team it makes sense for managers to accept the latter. When problems are examined in terms of the individuals involved, managers are better able to relate to the issues concerned with equal opportunities. If Jane has had six years of market research experience with the company and knows the industry inside out, but is contemplating leaving her job because she is pregnant, John, the manager may be more open to positive suggestions on how to negotiate flexible or part-time hours in order to retain her skills.

Examining the issues from both corporate and departmental level we can see that awareness raising in the initial stages must function in two ways:

1. Influencing the attitudes of top executives, especially those who have the power and responsibility for implementing policy. This is concerned with gaining acceptance of the principle that is right and just to create opportunities for women to take their place alongside men.
2. Identifying the problem in terms of wasted resources and recognising the economic sense of investing in women as a positive attribute for the future growth and efficiency of the company.

Cultural barriers

The company is comprised of a system of ideas, beliefs and values which have developed as part of its tradition. These values are largely dictated by top management whose goals and policy will influence how the company behaves. For change to occur these traditional ideas must be challenged at all levels in order to expose weaknesses and to introduce new ideas. For men and women working together this must begin by focusing on their roles in relation to their jobs and the organisation.

Managerial attitudes

Part of the process of change is to influence the traditional culture of the company which may not be predisposed to the natural changes taking place within society as a whole. For example, a survey of managers were asked what proportion of the population they considered to comprise the 'average' family, i.e. husband working, wife at home and two children. Estimates ranged between 25 to 40 per cent when in fact the real figure is 5 per cent. This serious mismatch between beliefs and reality highlights a common thread throughout organisations which tend to be inward looking. Changing the culture thus becomes a process of adjustment to the actual social and economic changes which are rapidly occurring in the marketplace.

Just as top managers are asked to examine their beliefs and attitudes towards women at work so too should managers at all other levels of operation be given the opportunity to express their views. Much of this work can be done in workshops which aim to:

(a) Examine individual attitudes and beliefs.

(b) Identify problems perceived in the way things operate.

(c) Relate current attitudes and practices to the aims of the organisation.

(d) Create a positive climate and the vision for change.

(e) Examine the means and resources to bring about change.

(f) Demonstrate the use of workshop training suitable for changing the attitudes of other employees.

On some of the courses we have run we have experimented to test the cultural attitudes towards men and women. We have asked both women and men to complete the following phrases:

Women are . . . .
Men are . . . .

Each course member completed this phrase ten times. The results made very interesting reading and told us a good deal about the attitudes and assumptions of both women and men. All the respondees held management roles, 50 per cent of them in personnel.

Women's view of women

The majority of women saw their own sex as caring, loving and understanding. A significant number of responses focused on personality traits and women see themselves as: affectionate, devoted, generous, gentle and generally considerate and aware of the needs of others. Although they can be emotionally strong they are physically softer (than men) with a degree of sensitivity and empathy. The roles that women fulfil varied from the more usual wives, mothers, sisters, daughters to workers, cooks, slaves, martyrs and sufferers! Not one woman saw another as filling the role of manager or leader. The more positive traits were down-to-earth, independent, confident, decisive, influential, adventurous, clean, tidy and efficient. The negative characteristics were devious, cynical, manipulative, scheming, lacking in assertiveness, lacking ambition and less powerful at work. Some are easily influenced, contented with too little and dependent on men.

The work-related characteristics represent good news to employers of women. They are dedicated, reliable, organised, practical, responsible, hard-working, tolerant, capable and fair. They will be loyal, honest, trustworthy, conscientious, dependable and committed to their work. They see themselves as thoughtful, wise, intelligent, efficient and good at teaching others.

Some women see themselves as evolving. Others describe themselves as: 'The new leaders of the world'! 'The power behind the men'! 'Fierce fighters in specific circumstances.' Most have a strong family orientation and see themselves as 'the binders of the family' or 'the centre of the family unit'.

One can see from the above lists how enduring are the roles which have been passed down from mother to daughter over the centuries. It is encouraging, however, to see evidence of change from 'caring and dependent on men' to 'the power behind the men and the real leaders of the world'.

Men's view of women

Men agree with women that women are physically weaker but emotionally stronger. There were a few direct contradictions. At one end of the scale for instance women are considered shy but at the other bossy, stubborn and domineering! Or women are better listeners than men yet conversely always talking!

On the positive side women are kind, considerate, tolerant, subtle and sociable. In the view of one man, somewhat patronising perhaps, women are grateful! Women are considered cleaner, better groomed and better dressed than their male counterparts.

The negative side of women's behaviour is seen as sly, devious, crafty and cunning. Women moan a lot, hold grudges longer and they can be vain and arrogant as well as bitchy and crude. At work women are seen as loyal, hard-working, more level-headed, professional and consistent than men. Some men described women as mentally equal to men and better managers overall. Women still fill the roles of wives and mothers and are generally thought to be more homely than men. Women are also seen as sexy, appealing, loving, soft-hearted and feminine. One man produced two identical lists for both women and men and made the following observation: 'there are differences in style in the way that men and women behave but as a generality because they are individuals they can be classed as broadly similar.'

Women's view of men

There were many adjectives describing men as the stronger sex and women see men as physically strong, definitely the stronger sex and stronger minded than women. Other adjectives used all give the feeling of strength, e.g. forceful, authoritative and arrogant, powerful, aggressive, assertive, determined, violent, loud and above all dominating.

Some women however see a softer side of men which is protective, generous, empathetic, loyal, caring, dependable, reliable, constant and human.

At work men are frequently seen as unsympathetic and unwilling to listen to problems, or even to listen at all! They are described as ambitious, dynamic and work oriented rather than people oriented. Some women feel that men have changed their attitude towards women. Another view is that they are 'blinkered and fail to see the reality of women' and that they are 'resistant to female careers'. In one view men are 'fighting desperately to retain their illusion as leaders'! We are warned that men are 'just not fair in job share'. There is no doubt whatever that men are career-minded, conditioned to be breadwinners, competitive, more powerful at work and they expect promotion and are good 'company' men.

There were some very telling phrases about the way men are in their leisure time: when they are not tinkering with the car, they are drinking or watching sport or glued in front of the television set. They are sexist, sex-mad and male chauvinists! Insecure, hypocritical, lazy and untidy, forgetful and disorganised, weak and childish! They are not 'fully participative members of the family unit' and tend to be 'reactionary in domestive roles'. They can be liberal with the truth, say one thing and practice another. The last and very telling word on men was 'desirable'.

Men's view of men

The observations under this heading were downright pithy but none the less cogent.

Once again the majority view was that men are strong, dominant and aggressive. They consider themselves better at physical work than women and in fact consider themselves hard working. They will push hard to achieve their aims.

There were some contradictions as in subtle–crude; generous–tight; energetic–lazy. The more negative traits are selfishness, impatience, unfaithful, smelly. The positive traits are athleticism, directness, calm, brave. Roles are husbands, fathers, people and individuals but again no leaders, directors or chairmen. Men do, however, see themselves as money-makers, a description not found under any other heading.

What conclusions can be reached from this thesaurus? That both women and men can be 'all things to all people'? That both sexes assume one role at work, another at home and several more in differing circumstances with different people? We undoubtedly adjust our behaviour several times in the course of a day, depending on the circumstances and the role we are playing at the time. Each sex, however, has to live with the stereotypes which persist whether we like it or not. A man is strong indeed if he admits that he is not comfortable with the aggressive dominant role prescribed for him. A woman will flagellate herself for not being sensitive and caring in a given situation. Both women and men are influenced by the role stereotypes pertinent to their sex and it is these entrenched attitudes which trainers and others, who see their role as catalytic, are trying to change.

We continued our exercise by asking both sexes how they would like the other to change and we received the following answers.

How do women need to change:

1. Women should have more confidence in their abilities. They should not feel less able to do a job than a man.
2. Women should stop gossiping and complaining to each other and get up and do something.
3. Women should be more independent, more ambitious and change their attitudes towards men.
4. Women should show less emotion in their workplace.
5. I would like women to stop fighting so aggressively for their rights and to use the skills they have to obtain them in a less conflicting manner.
6. Women should display their capabilities more, and to their own advantage. They should strive for recognition and acceptance.
7. Women need more equal opportunities but not necessarily preferential treatment.

How do men need to change:

1. Men should be more open to suggestion, i.e. that they are not always right! They should be prepared to listen.
2. I would like men to feel OK about showing their more vulnerable side.
3. I would like men to have a higher standard overall and not to look down on women or take them for granted.
4. I would like men to think they are less superior, to be more open-minded and less frightened of change.
5. Men need to be more aware of women's capabilities in the workplace and acknowledge that women and men must be able to have both a family and a career.
6. Men should be more aware of the value of women. Men should try to be more caring and be less remote. They should be more patient and approachable, listen to others and help or support them rather than hear and discuss and ignore.

General Conclusions

There are differences in the way women and men behave but as a generality because they are all individuals they can be classed as broadly similar. Perhaps one solution to the great divide is that each sex should appreciate the qualities that the other brings to the workplace and worry less about what sex they are.

One of the most difficult problems encountered in translating top management decisions into action can be the resistance of managers to change. This was highlighted in the 1986 report commissioned by the Equal Opportunities Commission on equal opportunity practice at British Rail. The study found that most managers interviewed were hostile to the principle of equal opportunity. If policy is imposed on managers then it will inevitably create resistance to change. The aim must always be to involve managers in the formulation of policy from the very beginning, using top management directives as an impetus for creating commitment rather than as directives on practice.

Women's attitudes and behaviour

Although much attention will be focused on the problems men may have in accepting full working partnerships with women, it should also be recognised that women too create their own barriers. Much of this can be attributed to their general lack of confidence which inhibits them from developing goals for advancement. Women are less likely to identify their potential and push themselves forward for training or promotion. They are less likely to express their needs or be assertive in their dealings within the workplace.

Part of this problem can be related to the lack of role models within the organisation where there are relatively few top female managers. Confidence is enhanced by being able to identify with the person who has just been promoted – 'If she can do it so can I.' We learn a great deal from those around us and if a woman is seen to be successful, despite similar constraints to other women, this will have a far stronger influence on her co-workers than a man in a similar position. If role models do not exist they can be developed through training pro- grammes which are designed to accelerate the progress of women with potential. (See Chapter 8.)

Women only workshops

Women can help each other a great deal in learning to recognise the barriers they create for themselves. Workshops designed to expose the barriers inherent in women's perceptions are extremely effective in challenging negative attitudes. For example, Sun Alliance ran a series of courses for women's development which, wherever possible, posed the question: 'What have you appreciated about yourself and the women you have just been working with?' During the programmes women were encouraged to build a personal vision for their future, one without self-imposed limits where they can achieve their full potential. Having visualised and described it to each other they began to identify the steps towards making it a reality. These workshops are followed up by regular meetings of small support groups where participants share time equally to speak about:

What is going well in my life?
What is difficult?
What do I need to do next?

Sun Alliance also ran women in management courses as part of their equal opportunities programme which offered some women the first opportunity to experience their personal power and potential as leaders. As a result, many of them have become directly involved in bringing about changes and a number have been promoted to more senior positions.

The Gatekeepers

Women in positions of authority can have a powerful influence on the progress of other women, both positive and negative. In this way they act as gatekeepers, capable of opening and closing access to help, advice and support. The open gatekeeper welcomes the opportunity to use her experience and insight to promote opportunities for women and encourage a corporate response to women's needs. She has the confidence to recognise that developing other women is no threat to her position. She also has the generosity to be prepared to give and act as an enabler for those she works with. In doing so she provides a valuable service to the company and all concerned.

There are also those women who, like many men, feel threatened by possible changes in their situation. This is especially true for the woman who has had to do things the hard way, proving that she is better than men of equivalent status to reach her position. She may resent the fact that proposals are in hand to speed up the progress for women that has taken her a long time to achieve. If she has had to make a choice between career or marriage and children, she may find it hard to accept that women can or should have help to do both if they so choose.

These women present barriers to progress unless they too are closely involved in the early stages of awareness raising. They too need to express their feelings, explore their attitudes and seek some reassurance. Most of all they need to be given a positive role with the recognition necessary to contribute positively to the changes which are needed. If they are chosen as advisers, mentors or facilitators at planning and development sessions this will encourage them to be creative about the process and gain their commitment.

The will to change

It is vital to the life of an equal opportunities programme that the will to change is sought from all, at all levels, in order for it to work.

Raising awareness of the problems inherent in a company's culture regarding the role of women is a strategy for developing the will to change. This is brought about by developing a questioning climate to examine all that is going on and why it is the case. This should lead to questions on whether it need necessarily be this way, what alternatives there are and whether the alternatives would be for the better. When agreement has been reached on what could be done to change, questions can be raised on how best to take action. Ideas on what resources will be needed should be sought and how these resources could be best used.

Involvement in discussing the issues and planning for change takes the form of action learning in the sense that the individuals involved take responsibility for their own part in the process. This sense of responsibility is required to motivate all to want to make the policy work rather than to resist it.

The will to change is concerned with motivation which is enhanced by:

Better working relationships
Wider opportunities
Greater recognition

These three factors form the basis of any equal opportunities plan. Using the questioning technique to explore these factors will reveal where possible blocks to motivation lie and in doing so solutions may become apparent.

Organisation climate questionnaire

One way to identify the strengths and weaknesses which lie within the organisation is by use of an organisation climate questionnaire. By comparing the responses given by both men and women it is possible to highlight areas of concern which can then act as a stimulus for the will to change. The use of a climate questionnaire performs both the task of raising awareness and identifying the problems generally and in relation to different departments within the organisation. If the questionnaire is employed prior to awareness workshops, the results can be used to stimulate discussion on ideas for change (see Appendix).

Organisational barriers

Organisational barriers usually present themselves in the form of time, money or resources. The lack of any one of these prevents the other two from being effective. Managers are generally preoccupied with the day-to-day running of their operations. They can neither afford their time nor the time of employees to give to training for which they can see no immediate tangible results. Questionnaires and workshops take valuable time and may be questionable in the eyes of managers who are sceptical about the notion of equal opportunities. In these circumstances it becomes very easy for a manager to find reasons why it is impossible to participate in a workshop. This has been said to be true of other similar organisational change programmes like a quality programme. Yet few managers would admit to having no commitment to quality. Clearly no programme will work unless it is given high priority since it has been said that time is a matter of priorities. Some things never get done because they never rise high enough on the list of priorities. Equal opportunity programmes, just like any other company policies, can only work if they are given high priority in terms of time and resources. Like all training programmes they should have targets for achievement which can be measured within time limits. If reaching these targets becomes the responsibility of individual managers with full accountability for success and failure built into appraisal systems then equal opportunities should be included on the list of top priorities.

Who is responsible

Implementation of an equal opportunities policy can only take place with the fullest authority and vigour to ensure it is mandatory for all employees. To appoint an equal opportunities officer without this backing is a pointless exercise. S/he may be able to produce excellent booklets, suggestions and advice but these, in themselves, will do little to achieve the real change in values necessary.

Although ultimate responsibility for the development programme may lie with one person, responsibility must also be delegated to those who are in a position of power to have a direct influence on both managers and staff. This power net may also include those who are in a position of influence, like the Personnel Manager, union officials and supervisors as well as senior managers. Delegation of such authority must take account of managers and supervisors who clearly demonstrate their commitment to the process and who will actively pursue the principles contained in the policy. These key characters will become change agents for the organisation and should form a working party to examine the key issues. They too must participate in an awareness programme with the Equal Opportunities Officer to form a consensus view on what problems exist and what changes are necessary. They will want to identify those areas where change could take immediate effect without causing major difficulties. Ideally these interventions will be tied to the process of awareness raising like courses on interviewing techniques which begin by examining inbuilt biases which are part of our conditioning.

Taking time

Real awareness raising is a slow process and it could take several years before the effects of a programme permeate all departments of an organisation. Resistance and acceptance of the principles of equality will vary widely according to the age, sex and personal histories of individual employees. Some may never change and their prejudices will only disappear on their retirement. Others will pay lip-service to the policy initially but hopefully this will be converted to an inner conviction once the practice of equality becomes a norm. The role of the equal opportunities manager is to identify those who can help bring about a more positive awareness of the issues as the starting point for change.

4   Making a Start

The name may vary: Equal Opportunities Commission, Equal Opportunities Council, Equal Opportunities Unit or even Ministry for Women's Rights but each member state of the European Community has a body responsible for ensuring that the law guaranteeing the equal treatment of women and men is enforced. These departments are staffed by experts – 98 per cent of them women – who are trained in the interpretation of the legislative framework pertinent to their own country.

In Denmark equal opportunities advisers were appointed to all the employment offices as far back as 1981. These officers have the task of detecting and eliminating cases of discrimination in occupational guidance and placement. They are also involved in the activities of management committees of the local employment offices, in which the two sides of industry, local authorities and education, co-operate.

The work of the French equal opportunities agencies became rationalised and specialised with the assignment of *déléguées en égalité* to the factory and shop inspectorates. These advisers check the annual report which all firms employing more than 50 workers in their area of jurisdiction are required by law to submit. The first statistical part of these reports compares the situation of female and male workers. The second part, in which both the management and the works council are required to express their views, contains proposals for measures to reduce the under-representation of any discrimination against women in certain areas.

Many member states have decided that public employers should perform a pilot function where equal opportunities are concerned. Several federal German Länder have consequently drawn up plans for the advancement of women in the public service, with the aim of recruiting, training and promoting more women in the areas where they are under-represented.

Our own Equal Opportunities Commission was set up at the end of 1975 following the Equal Opportunities Act. Their budget of £3.8 million is small for such an influential body. The Commission for Racial

Equality, for instance, has a budget of around £10 million to focus on 10 per cent of the population. The Equal Opportunities Commission's research profile: 'Women and Men in Britain' identified that the industrial distribution of employment is more influenced by gender than by ethnic origin. The EOC has three major aims:

1. To promote equal opportunities generally and this work includes an educational and consciousness raising role.
2. To eliminate sex discrimination totally by using the legal powers at its disposal.
3. To prepare reports and recommendations for the Home Office on the effectiveness of the current acts and to male requests for amendments to existing acts. They will take up and fight a discrimination complaint if it establishes a legal precedent or if the case is too complex for the individual to fight alone. They can offer verbal or written advice, they have a wide range of publications and visual aids and their sphere of influence extends from the classroom to the company.

Much of the focus of the EOC has been on the compatibility of family and working life. Part-time work, for example, is seen as a transitional solution for women returning to work after maternity leave. They advocate that working hours should be commensurate with family needs. They have recommended special discrimination in favour of women on training schemes, particularly those that assist women into managerial roles or areas of work previously dominated by men. They have made recommendations on the equalising of the pension age between men and women and have been active in consumer affairs, for example, insurance policies and mortgage agreements which discriminate against women.

One of the EOC's more recent initiatives is the Equality Exchange. This is a forum for organisations committed to working to achieve equal opportunities for women and men in employment. Membership is open to organisations which are committed to becoming equal opportunities employers or who advise employers on personnel matters or provide training for employers. The forum facilitates the exchange of information and experience by holding meetings, conferences and workshops and establishing networks. The role of the EOC in this context is to keep members informed on policy, research and legal developments in equal opportunities. There is a parallel education network to which 74 local education authorities belong.

The EOC is involved in major Positive Action projects with the Metropolitan Police and the National Health Service and in 50 other training courses. The threat of legal action, however, continues to be a persuasive lever in enabling the Commission to resolve cases without having to go to tribunal or court. In 1987, over 1000 cases were resolved in this way. In the same year there were 33 preliminary investigations, which resulted in voluntary change without the need to proceed to formal enforcement action.

In spite of the fact that the equal opportunity laws and the EOC have been working hard to advance the cause of women for the past 13 years, research into the progress of women in large companies shows that employers are failing to get to grips with sexual discrimination. Much of the problem hinges around a 'glass ceiling' for women. This consists of a web of management myths and values which suggest that women are not suited for senior jobs. The glass ceiling was first identified in America by Anne Morrison, a director of the Centre for Creative Leadership in North Carolina. Morrison and her team made a three-year study of the progress of 76 top female executives in America's biggest companies. The results were compared with a similar study of male executives. This study revealed two barriers that women encounter during their progress up the corporate ladder. The first is at general manager level; the second at senior level.

The women's progress was slowed because their companies forced them to perform to higher standards than men. This is because companies believe it is risky to promote women to senior positions. The companies also put greater pressures on women to develop an acceptable image and management style. Some 38 per cent of women compared with 5 per cent of men, failed to get to the top because of poor image. Fifty per cent of women failed because they were too ambitious compared with 10 per cent of men. Twenty-five per cent of women were not ambitious enough compared with 10 per cent of men. It appears therefore that in order to approach the highest levels women are expected to have more strengths and fewer faults than their male counterparts.

For at least a decade now research, similar to that just quoted, has been carried out in a number of organisations to identify the reasons why women are not progressing up the corporate ladder. In some cases the impetus has come from outside the organisation from Training Agency sponsored schemes, from National Conferences, via encouragement from one of the many women's networks or from an external consultant with the needs of women at heart. There is a wealth of material, books, training packages and reports which are available from the Training Agency or direct from some of the women's networks.

The difficulty for many organisations is the translation of theoretical good practice into corporate policy. An excellent blueprint for action is the Littlewoods organisation which won the Women in Management Award for the best Equal Opportunity Policy in 1987. This organisation was started in 1923 by Sir John Moores CBE. Originally a football pools firm it now employs a total of 35,000 women and men and has three major divisions: Home Shopping, Chain Stores and Pools. The company felt that having an EO policy was not enough to help the company achieve genuine equality of opportunity. They recognised that there are both organisational and personal barriers which prevented many talented women from rising to senior positions. Twenty-eight thousand of the total workforce are women, as well as the majority of the customers, but women were scarcely represented in middle and senior management and thus effectively cut off from key decision-making processes.

The crucial decision for Littlewoods was to introduce a positive action programme to give teeth to its EO policy. They gave a firm commitment to ensure that women, black employees and disabled staff, together with other ethnic minority groups, were fairly represented at all levels in the company within five years. This commitment differs from many other organisations in that all levels of staff were included instead of a few high fliers. Littlewoods also considered that target setting would be compatible with commercial criteria for promotion and explained to staff that the targets meant more women would be promoted on the basis of their ability and not their sex. This is perhaps the most crucial aspect of the company aims. Instead of demanding that women should be better than men or rejecting the female management style and thus precipitating failure, they have made it clear to all their employees that the person promoted is the best for the job.

In order to achieve this radical change in their organisational attitude the company set up an Equal Opportunities Unit by appointing an EO manager (with specific responsibility for gender), a training officer and a race officer. The unit reports to the chief executive and its work is monitored quarterly by an EO committee consisting of senior managers, mainly employed at director level. The committee is chaired by John Moores who says 'Equal opportunities is not only fair, it makes sound business sense.'

The fundamental change in the organisational policy initially got a mixed reception from the predominantly male management team. A few were genuinely enthusiastic; some expressed scepticism and others were downright hostile. Over a two-year period, however, confidence in the company's programme increased and now people at all levels want to be associated with the company's progressive policies for women.

A wonderful example of the grass-roots effect of this kind of commitment to the training and development of staff at all levels is illustrated by the story of Amrit Sokhi. Amrit is currently employed as a departmental manager at a West End store in London. She began her career with Littlewoods as a Saturday assistant and is loud in her praise of Littlewoods managers who are at pains to identify young talent. She hopes that by moving into a training job she will be able to help other young women to progress with the company.

Following the introduction of the EO programme the percentage of women has risen in all levels of management. Table 3 gives an indication of the rise and the targets.

Table 3 Women in management 1985–1987

		1985		1987		1991 target	
	Zone	Nos	%	Nos	%	Nos	%
Director/Associate Director/Senior Executive	1–3	2	2.60	3	4.16	8	10
Senior management	4	3	1.85	12	5.90	24	15
Middle management	5	38	10.00	70	16.00	133	35
Junior/Middle management	6	112	21.70	182	27.60	258	50
Junior management	7	275	49.65	343	54.00	no target	
Supervisory	8–9	1487	64.90	1641	65.96	no target	

There has been a pronounced increase in the number of women in management training. In 1985 they took under a third of the places on trainee management schemes, by 1987 the percentage had risen to just over 50 per cent. Special initiatives such as child-care provision, improved maternity leave, paid leave for family reasons, job-sharing and career break schemes are currently being considered. Here again it was felt that these initiatives had to be placed within the structure of a broadly based EO programme to avoid favouring just a few senior women executives. Every single one of Littlewoods employees received a leaflet advising them of the EO programme, their right of access to the code of practice and to information and advice from the EO unit. The Code of Practice was also distributed to the company's 5000 managers.

Both women and men receive training in EO law and good practice in selection and recruitment. The company has taken steps to improve the education, training and development of all the women in the organisation. The programme for 1988 includes assertiveness training, women managers' meetings and a poster campaign promoting the role of women in Littlewoods.

This kind of effort provides very positive pay-offs. Word spreads rapidly about the quality of employers in an area and this encourages recruiting. Job placements at Littlewoods are regularly sought and provided, the computer division is particularly popular.

When a major employer in any industry sets this kind of precedent, other employers can be stimulated to do the same.

The National Westminster Bank was the first of the five big banks to operate a 'career break and returner scheme', other banks followed their example. In 1988 the Midland Bank opened the first of its work-place crèches in Crawley, another is planned for Sheffield with more to follow. Midland Bank also offers flexible working to encourage women with young families to come back to work.

The starting point for an equal opportunity programme

The first step towards more effective utilisation of the entire work-force is the formulation of an equal opportunity policy. It is essential to gain commitment to the policy at board level and to announce this commitment to all employees. To ensure that the policy is carried out it is advisable to assign responsibility to a senior executive. He/she will be involved in planning and monitoring the policy, for putting it into effect and will be expected to report back to the board on progress at regular intervals. Trade unions might well wish to become involved and may allocate responsibility to one of their members, depending on their structures and procedures in a particular work-place.

A model Equal Opportunity Policy has been produced by the EOC and is set out below.

A model equal opportunity policy

1. *Introduction*

   1.1 This company (authority or organisation) considers it desirable to produce a statement of policy on equal opportunity in employment to provide the necessary encouragement and guidance to staff to implement our policy. This document sets out our policy. It must be strictly adhered to by all managers (except where there are legal limitations on employment to particular posts). Disciplinary procedure may be used in the case of breach of our policy.

2. *Definitions*

2.1 In this policy 'discrimination' means discrimination where a person is treated less favourably on grounds of sex or marital status, as defined in the Sex Discrimination Act 1975.

2.2 In this policy 'indirect discrimination' means the imposition of a requirement or condition which is applied or would be applied equally to persons not of the same sex or marital status but

(i) which is such that the proportion of persons of the same sex and marital status who can comply with it is considerably smaller than the proportion of persons not of that group who can comply with it;
(ii) which cannot be shown to be justified irrespective of sex, marital status of the person to whom it is applied;
(iii) which is to the detriment of the individual concerned because he/she cannot comply with it.

2.3 In this policy the company (authority or organisation) includes any employee, whether full-time or part-time or on temporary employment to the Company, who acts on behalf of the Company.

3. *General statement of policy*

3.1 We believe that our policy and practice are a means of maximising the effective use of human resources in the company's (authority or organisation's) and the employees' best interests.

3.2 All members of staff employed by the company (authority or organisation) and all applicants for employment will be given equal opportunity irrespective of their sex and marital status in all aspects of employment and training, e.g. in their access to posts and in terms of the benefits on which employment is normally available in this company (authority or organisation). The company (authority or organisation) is committed not only to the letter of the law, but also to the promotion of equality of opportunity in all fields.

3.3 Application of collective agreements and the operation of recruitment, training and promotion policies to all individuals will be on the basis of job requirements and the individual's ability and fitness for work.

3.4 Staff employed by the company (authority or organisation) shall be made aware of the provisions for this policy. This may be done, for example, by means of advertisements, job descriptions, application forms, posters, training courses and handbooks for appropriate managerial and supervisory staff.

3.5 All key personnel involved in management, selection and dealing with the public shall be given training and guidance in the law and organisational policy, their own personal liability under the law and the nature of discrimination.

4. *Possible pre-conceptions*

4.1 In the application of the equal opportunity policy, it is essential that managers guard against discrimination on the basis of possible assumptions that individuals, because of their sex and marital status possess characteristics which would make them unsuitable for employment. Examples of such assumptions might be:

(i) Lack of commitment to work.
(ii) Have outside commitments which would interfere with work.
(iii) Possess poor mental/physical ability.
(iv) Produce an anticipated unfavourable reaction of other staff and members of the public.
(v) Be unsuitable for the job because of the feeling that certain types of work are only suitable for a member of the opposite sex of single status.
(vi) Be unable to supervise.
(vii) Possess limited career intentions.
(viii) Be unwilling to undertake training.

4.2 Age limits for entry to training schemes should not be unnecessarily restrictive to exclude certain groups of staff.

4.3 All staff involved in interviewing shall be trained to ensure that selection is made on an objective basis and that encouragement is given to women (or men) to take full advantage of training opportunities where in the past they have not been sufficiently confident to do so.

5. *Terms and conditions of service and facilities*

5.1 The company (authority or organisation) will not discriminate on the basis of sex or marital status in the provision of general staff facilities and benefits.

6. *Monitoring*

6.1 The Personnel Officer(s) will be nominated as the person(s) responsible for monitoring the effectiveness of the equal opportunity policy, with overall responsibility for its implementation and supervision remaining with the Personnel Director.

6.2 All aspects of Personnel policies and procedures shall be kept under review to ensure that they do not operate against equal opportunities and an analysis made of the sex and marital status of employees in relation to their employment within the company (authority or organisation).

6.3 Where it appears that any employees/applicants are not being offered equal opportunities, the circumstances will be investigated by management to see if there are any policies or criteria which exclude or discourage employees and, if so, whether these policies and criteria are justifiable.

Appropriate action will be taken where necessary to redress the effects of any policy or criteria which are found to have unjustifiably limited the provision of equal opportunities.

6.4 This equal opportunity policy will be reviewed from time to time by the appropriate body.

7. *Grievances and Victimisation*

7.1 Particular care will be taken to deal effectively with any complaints of discrimination and sexual harrassment which should be pursued through the Grievance Procedure.

7.2 The Sex Discrimination Act provides protection for individuals who have done anything in good faith by reference to the Sex Discrimination or Equal Pay Acts.

An equal opportunity policy must go beyond a statement of commitments. It should pave the way for the detailed practices and procedures to carry it out. Where there are recognised trade unions, it is essential that they are involved at the planning stage. Whether the organisation sets up an equal opportunity committee or, as in Littlewoods a small department, it is important for everyone involved to understand that the views of women and men from all sections of the work-force should be adequately considered.

Before discrimination can be rectified it is essential to identify if it exists and where it is happening. A detailed analysis of the distribution of women and men within the organisation will show their positions by grade, skill and pay within each department. If the distributions are significantly different it is important to examine the reasons. If the personnel policies of an organisation have been discriminatory or if those who implement policies have prejudiced attitudes, this can create low expectations in the sex that has been disadvantaged.

Personnel policies should be examined to see if there is any good reason why only men or women are engaged in particular types of work. Policies which are apparently equal can produce unequal effects and can therefore be indirectly discriminatory. An example of this might be the insistence on mobility or shift working. There are inherent feelings

about what constitutes 'women's work' and the jobs that are traditionally 'male'. A minor furore was created recently in a public body in
Birmingham when the Equal Opportunities Officer recruited a young
man as a 'temp' to operate the word processor. The men in the
department protested that the work was 'women's work' and they felt
that their sex had been grossly insulted by employing a man to carry it
out. Their feelings had nothing to do with the young man's performance
(which was excellent) and everything to do with inherited prejudice.

The EO policy will fail if key personnel do not understand the
implications of the statements made within it. It is advisable to brief all
managers, particularly those who are responsible for work opportunities and career progression. It is crucial to include all those who have
contact with job applications; telephonists, receptionists and secretaries
– all of whom can act as gate-keepers.

Recruitment and selection

The letter on p.58 appeared in the *Evening Standard* in November,
1988. The interviewer in question was making some remarkably arrogant assumptions about his male colleagues. Are we really to believe
that the current UK male workforce is composed of would be Don
Juans with eyes perenially roving in search of still more sexual satisfaction – we doubt it. And what about recruiting attractive men? Will they
be doomed to similar forms of harrassment from their female colleagues? Again this is doubtful.

The law states that every job must be open equally to women and men
who have the required qualifications except where an exception is
provided by the Sex Discrimination Act. Section 7 of the Act gives a list
of circumstances in which sex may be acceptable as a 'genuine
occupational qualification'.

Job advertisements

Job advertisements should neither state nor imply in any way that the
job is open only to applicants of one sex. If, however, the criteria in
section 7 applies this should be clearly stated in the job advertisement.
The Equal Opportunities Commission has the authority to apply to a
county court (a sheriff court in Scotland) for an injunction to restrain
people from publishing advertisements which are discriminatory.

The exception to the above rule is allowed under section 48 of the
Act, this allows for positive action and recruitment advertising. In

Attracting a male prejudice

R ecently a young female engineering graduate attended for an interview at a company – a large multi-national. Despite the fact that she appeared to have all the necessary qualifications, she was refused a position.

Some days later it transpired that the interviewer was of the opinion that she was so attractive that her male colleagues would never have got any work done had she been offered a job.

What chance do women have in succeeding in science and engineering when male managers retain such childish prejudices? – **James O'Donnell, Church Road, Mitcham, Surrey.**

certain circumstances the Sex Discrimination Act allows employers to encourage job applications from women or men for jobs which can be done by either sex. This is a form of positive action used to counteract the effects of past discrimination. It would be used for jobs where at any time during the preceding 12 months there were no persons of the sex in question among those doing that work or the number of persons doing that work was comparatively small.

Before placing such an advertisement employers need to be sure exactly what the balance of the sexes is among their employees who are doing the particular kind of job to be advertised. Although section 48 also allows employers to encourage one sex to train for or apply for certain jobs, for example to encourage men to train for a career in nursing; it does not allow anyone to discriminate by sex when it comes to selecting who will be recruited or promoted. It is not lawful to try to correct an imbalance of the sexes in the workforce by seeking to operate a quota system. The Act requires that appointments should be made on merit, not sex, and that applicants must be treated equally when it comes to selection. Looking back to the earlier part of this chapter and employment practices within the Littlewoods organisation, the setting of quotas can only be achieved if the women selected to fill the vacancies are the best qualified for the job.

In practice it is not lawful for large employers to have a policy of encouraging applicants from one sex for every vacancy advertised. A general statement encouraging women cannot be used in large advertisements containing several different kinds of jobs, in some of which women are already well represented. Job titles, headlines and illustrations need to be used with care. Nothing in the advertisements must give the impression that one sex will be treated more favourably than the other.

The following examples indicate the type of advertisements which are acceptable and recommended by the EOC and those which are not considered good practice.

These are acceptable examples

ECOLOCHEM Ltd.

Wo aro ono of Europo'c largoet industrial companies and we have vacancies for junior laboratory technicians at our Northwest refinery. If you have good CSE or "O" level passes in English, Mathematics and a science why not consider a job in the petro-chemical industry?

At present few of our lab. technicians are women. Applications from women as well as men will therefore be welcome. (Section 48, Sex Discrimination Act).

Graduate Engineers Wanted – Male/Female

BRIDGEFORD COMPONENTS

The company has no women currently employed in this field and would particularly welcome applications from suitably qualified women.

These are bad examples

These advertisements are unlawful because they encourage women to apply for every job, regardless of the requirements of section 48 of the SDA.

Note that, if the statements in these two advertisements had been broad ones about equality of opportunities generally, without specifically encouraging one sex, the advertisements would have been lawful.

ONE HOUSING WORKER
(SHORT-LIFE TEAM)

to be responsible for the day-to-day management of our new short-life properties. Experience in housing management essential, particularly in either short-life or shared housing.

TWO HOUSING WORKERS
(PERMANENT PROPERTY TEAM)

One of whom must be female, (Sex Discrimination Act 1975 (Part 2,7(2)(e)), to manage a number of mixed and women-only hostels. Experience in housing management is essential; a background in social work and/or group work with special needs would be an advantage. ✓

Sandyheath Housing Association is committed to a policy of equal opportunities and positively welcomes applications from women, members of ethnic minorities, particularly from the Asian community, gay men and lesbians and people with disabilities. ✗

Another unlawful 'positive action' advertisement

TORCHESTER BOROUGH COUNCIL

Please quote appropriate number when requesting an application form.

Environmental Health Officer   789635/24
A vacancy exists in the Environmental Health Department for an experienced Officer.

Assistant Engineer (Main Drainage)   789635/35
To survey existing system, and design new and remedial drainage and civil engineering works.

Word Processing Operator   623487/87
To work in Housing Department. Minimum of RSA II typing and audio experience is essential.

REF: 583842
Secretary   583842/56
A vacancy has arisen in the Legal Department for an experienced secretary. Advanced typing (pref. RSA III) and shorthand/audio skills more valuable than experience of legal work.

REF: 594367
Teachers
Scale 1   Class teacher (temporary post) Carlton Junior
Scale 2   Domestic Science (Job Share available) Croxley High
Scale 2   English to 'A' level Croxley High
Scale 2   Mathematics to 'O' level Dunstans High

**WE PARTICULARLY WELCOME APPLICATIONS
FROM WOMEN FOR ALL THESE POSTS**

Genuine occupational qualifications

In section 7(2) of the Sex Discrimination Act there is a list of Genuine Occupational Qualifications (GOQs) which specify when a job can lawfully be restricted to one sex; for example, to preserve decency or privacy; or when a woman or man is needed to take part in a play. Sometimes advertisers feel that to encourage applicants of one sex is less provocative than to rely on a GOQ, even when the duties required justify a GOQ. This creates problems, however, because in such cases the objective is not to encourage the under-represented sex, but to keep the jobs in question single-sex. In these circumstances, statements merely encouraging applications from one sex should not be used instead of GOQs.

Internal documentation

Section 38(3) of the Act refers to 'sexually connotated' job titles and states that 'use of a job description with a sexual connotation such as "waiter" or "salesgirl" will be taken as an intention to discriminate unless there is an indication to the contrary'. Where equivalent feminine and masculine job titles exist, for example, waiter/waitress it is probably best to use both. Where there are no feminine or masculine equivalents it is best to change all sexually connotated job titles in all company documentation as a basic precaution against making mistakes, e.g. 'storeman' becomes 'storekeeper'; 'matron' becomes 'senior nursing officer'; 'cameraman' becomes 'camera operator'. It is recommended that all the language used in job descriptions and staff handbooks should be checked carefully to avoid making elementary mistakes which can be construed as discriminatory. Employers frequently maintain that although they offer equality of opportunity, women just do not apply for the vacant jobs.

There are a number of ways in which, intentionally or unintentionally, women are deterred or prevented from applying for vacancies. If internal advertisements for vacancies are placed in a part of the organisation which is restricted to men then it follows that women will never even see them or if a vacancy notice is written entirely in male terms, 'he will be expected to', 'he will require' and so on.

A university professor wrote a letter to a colleague at another university, asking that 'the right man' be recommended as Director of a development project. The addressee put the letter up on the notice-board where it became the subject of a formal complaint to the EOC by qualified women students. A newsletter was sent to all members of a farming organisation advertising a vacancy in one of their branches and suggesting that members or their sons might be interested.

An employer advertising for casual jobs distributed leaflets to local houses on an estate offering full and part-time work to women but not to men. The men complained to the EOC and were quite right to do so. A hand-written notice posted outside an umbrella factory stated: 'Part-time packers required, no mums with young children'.

From 7 February 1987, the Sex Discrimination Act was amended to include all employers, previously those with five or fewer employers were exempt. This change was necessary in order that the UK could comply with a ruling of the European Court of Justice and so even if you have only one employee the Sex Discrimination Act applies to you.

The benefits of good personnel practice are that the company will employ people who are best suited to the job and this will be reflected in the way in which the jobs are carried out. In a 'good' company all personnel will be trained to do their jobs and training will be continuously updated to meet the changing needs of the organisation. People will then be motivated to contribute to the success of the business.

Selection procedures

Job applicants must all be treated fairly during the interview. The questions asked should relate to the needs of the job. If the job involves working unsocial hours, extensive travel or frequent moves it will be necessary to ask questions to see whether personal circumstances will be affected by the needs of the job. These questions, however, should be asked objectively and should be asked of men as well as women applicants.

Employers sometimes forget that men have wives and families who may be affected by frequent job moves. No family, for instance, will welcome a relocation at a time which is crucial to the children's education. Many organisations now recognise that frequent uprooting of the family is a very stressful experience and are paying greater consideration to the timing of career moves.

All job applicants should be looked at as individuals and not as female or male. We now have women driving trains and buses, Jaguar cars appointed a woman welder in 1987. Sian Holmes was the first woman to qualify as a chartered minerals surveyor and is the only woman in a field of 700. Men have been members of the nursing profession for several years and there are also a number of male secretaries. One man made his debut on national television as an 'Avon

Lady', a job at which he is extremely successful. As the barriers between 'women's work' and 'men's work' are removed there are fewer excuses for discrimination except the GOQs mentioned earlier in this chapter.

Women and men must be offered equal training opportunities and, whatever the job, the career path for both should be similar. Some interesting research was carried out by Marina Aivaliotis for the Hotel and Catering Training Board looking at the different career paths of women and men. Marina found that real barriers existed for women, particularly those trying to make inroads into jobs less associated with women. The training for women was usually restricted to specific areas of work, particularly personnel, training and sales. The men received a much broader based management training giving them increased scope for movement, either within the industry or to other areas. The women interviewed exhibited no positive evidence of long-term career planning at the beginning of their working life. It was felt therefore that women needed more constructive guidance than they actually received on the different career options that were open to them.

The employees in the hotel and catering industry who attained senior management positions, whether male or female, had all taken the time to make long-term career plans and had pursued career moves which were 'sideways and upwards' giving a breadth of experience of all aspects of the industry. One woman who was able to progress to be general manager of a London hotel had actually compiled for herself a training programme and pressed her employer to implement it. A man in a similar position had put age targets on his career plan, for example to become a hotel general manager by the time he was 31.

Appraisal systems

An effective appraisal system is based on the performance of the individual in his or her job. The most effective managers have a regular monitoring procedure which will culminate in the more formal appraisal interview. Ideally there will be no nasty shocks to administer during the appraisal interview because the manager will have adopted a coaching and counselling role as part of his/her strategy. We have found in our experience of running management development programmes for both sexes that most managers dislike criticising a subordinate. We overcome this problem by suggesting that constructive criticism is providing the employee with valuable feedback on their performance which will be particularly useful if accompanied by positive help and advice on improving that performance. This way, we argue, managers can help their subordinates to progress whilst paving the way for a positive appraisal interview. This process of continuing feedback helps employees to see themselves in a more objective light and raise their awareness of their strengths and weaknesses. It provides a basis for learning and an opportunity to implement a change in performance in the future. For managers it plays a vital part in continuing to improve and maintain standards. If feedback is avoided the employee gets the feeling that their performance has gone unnoticed and that their boss simply is not interested. It is remarkable that many managers feel uncomfortable about giving praise and are consequently sparing with it in spite of the fact that most of us respond positively to a genuine appreciation of our efforts.

The more formal appraisal interview should be totally free of sex bias; the employee is, or is not, performing adequately. One young woman graduate working in the hotel industry was advised during the course of an appraisal interview to 'wear a bit more make-up' she supposed to make herself more attractive to the customers. This is a good example of biased appraisal.

Job evaluation

This is a system of comparing different jobs to provide a basis for a grading and pay structure. The aim is to evaluate the job and not the job holder. Non-discriminatory job evaluation should lead to a payment system within which work of equal value receives equal pay regardless of sex. The *ACAS Booklet No. 1 – Job Evaluation* is recommended reading for anyone who is considering setting up a job evaluation scheme. Any scheme which has been in use for several years should be examined for discriminatory evidence. As we saw from Chapter 1, recent cases on equal value legislation make it essential to ensure that fair comparisons are made between jobs of different character.

It is recognised good practice to involve a representative sample of people from the spread of jobs covered by a scheme in discussions and committees. It is assumed that they will be the best people to represent their own interests. A participative approach will ensure easier acceptance of the scheme and resolving of difficulties at an early stage. There should be a fair representation of women in relation to the proportions in the workforce and in the jobs spectrum. This will help to reduce the probability of sex bias.

Research has shown that the chairmen of Job Evaluation Committees can be very influential in determining the outcome of the committees' considerations. It is therefore important that the chair should be selected not just for their knowledge of job evaluation but also because they are unbiased and concerned to ensure the procedures do not result in discrimination against jobs performed by women.

Job descriptions written to an agreed format enable the jobs to be assessed according to a common standard. An acceptable format will contain the following elements: job title; relationships at work, for example the kind and degree of supervision to be given and received, the nature and extent of co-operation with other workers; a short summary of the primary functions of the job; a description of specific duties of the job showing the approximate percentage of time spent on each duty and the extent of discretion or responsibility in relation to each duty; the job requirements listed under headings used for the subsequent job evaluation procedure, for example, skill, responsibility, mental effort, physical effort.

The preparation of job descriptions involves at least three people: the employee who does the job or a representative employee, that person's supervisor or manager and the job analyst or the person responsible for the procedures. The analyst will need to be aware of different titles which are used for the jobs of women and men who are doing essentially the same work. This has resulted historically in a status difference, reflected in a pay difference which is based on sex discrimination and not on the content of the work done. Examples are:

MALE JOB TITLE	FEMALE JOB TITLE
Salesman	Shop assistant
Assistant manager	Manager's assistant
Office manager	Typing supervisor
Chef	Cook

It is recognised that in some circumstances the different job titles are applied to jobs which are essentially different. They are only discriminatory where they are applied to the same job and result in different status or pay levels. Provision is normally made for a formal appeals procedure to deal with cases where the employee believes that their job has been unfairly evaluated. A representative committee is usually set up and it should be trained in job evaluation and sex discrimination. All employees should be informed that care has been taken not to discriminate against employees of either sex via the job evaluation scheme and that the appeals procedure can be used if they feel that they have been wrongly graded.

If a case of unlawful discrimination is taken to tribunal the process of the job evaluation scheme will be examined as part of the evidence of discrimination. The whole point of becoming an equal opportunity employer, however, is to implement such good, unbiased recruitment, selection, training and employment practices that this situation never arises.

5 Gaining Help

In the wake of equal opportunities legislation came many schemes and initiatives which can be categorised as affirmative positive action programmes. The majority of these innovative training initiatives were funded by the Training Agency or by the European Social Fund. It cannot be stressed too highly, however, that the individual programmes were started by committed individuals who wanted to make a real contribution to the progress of women during the last quarter of the twentieth century.

Some of the Industrial Training Boards appointed women to be responsible for women's training initiatives in particular industries. The early schemes were normally grant aided. This fact alone indicates the reluctance prevalent in the major industries to take positive action in favour of women. It has taken a decade and the beginnings of demographic changes for companies to appreciate the value of attracting women into jobs which have status, career development possibilities and the added bonus of training or development programmes. Even now the majority of companies put far more effort into recruitment than into retention of staff in general and women in particular and a good deal of work has still to be carried out in this area. In December 1988 the government introduced an anti-discrimination and deregulation Employment Bill designed specifically to sweep away some of the remaining differences between the employment of women and men in Britain. This is an official recognition that with the falling birth rate the role of women in the next decade will be increasingly important to fill the gap in the employment market created by fewer school leavers.

The Bill aims to promote equality of opportunity in employment and vocational training and is designed to meet EEC obligations by amending or repealing most of the legislation that still discriminates in employment and training matters between women and men. Six of the clauses in the Bill deal specifically with sex discrimination and amend the provisions of the Sex Discrimination Act 1975 which have allowed discriminatory requirements in earlier legislation to prevail. A good example is the mining industry where women were prevented from pursuing careers in management or engineering because of restrictions introduced in the nineteenth century. The only remaining restrictions are allowed for health and safety reasons. Protection will be retained so that women are not exposed to radiation or lead which might affect the health of an unborn child. There are also restrictions which prohibit women from working on board ships or aircraft and on women returning to work in factories within four weeks of childbirth.

The main points of the Bill which directly affect women are as follows:

1. Academic appointments in university colleges to be restricted to women where this is required at present.
2. Exemptions for women to protect them from working in situations which put them at risk, e.g. affecting unborn children.
3. Repeals the existing restrictions on women working in mines and quarries and cleaning machinery in factories by extending to men the prohibition, at a mine or quarry, of lifting loads 'so heavy as to be likely to cause injury'.
4. Head teachers in schools and colleges to be restricted to members of a religious order where such a restriction is contained in the trust deed or other relevant instrument.
5. Removes the differences whereby men may at present receive statutory redundancy payments up to age 65 and women up to only age 60. Where there is a 'normal retiring age' for the job in question which is below 65 and is non-discriminatory, the entitlement of both sexes is to be restricted to that age. In all other cases women's entitlement is to be extended to age 65 in line with that of men.

The role of the Equal Opportunities Commission has been described in detail in the previous chapter and all queries regarding breaches of statutory legislation should be referred to them. Other agencies are concerned with promoting equal opportunities for women. These are described below and a complete list of names and addresses is provided at the end of the book.

The Women and Training Group

This is a national network initially set up and funded by the Training Agency. It was set up in 1979 to address some of the training issues for women which was then a new and untapped area. Since then the group has expanded its work and audiences and has shared the experience gained through workshops and publications with a wide range of organisations and individuals. The aims of the group are to:

1. Consider areas of need and stimulate innovation in training for mature and young women and to facilitate co-operation on the development of projects.
2. Provide forums for appropriate bodies and individuals to exchange information and ideas on training opportunities for women.
3. Seek liaison and co-operation with the broad spectrum of people involved or interested in training opportunities for women.
4. Seek to raise and maintain awareness, generate interest, influence and involve those not yet committed to the development of women through training, as well as maintaining the commitment of those actively involved.

The group aims to encourage the development of women through organising conferences and workshops. It identifies approaches to meeting the training and development needs of women and disseminates information and experience of successful strategies, techniques and methods. A newsletter *Women and Training News* is published three times a year and is circulated to employers, trade unions, educational and training organisations and interested individuals. It shares practical experience in training women and demonstrates by example that women can be trained for, and successfully employed in, non-traditional occupations at all levels of responsibility and skill.

At the time of writing membership of the group is free and members receive the newsletter and information about group events. This situation will, however, change in the future. At the centre of the group's activities is a small group of experienced women's training practitioners who meet regularly to develop the group strategy and plan events. It says much for the commitment of these women that their time is given freely and regularly on a monthly basis.

There is a network of regional groups, twelve in all, in strategic parts of the UK. The existence of these groups depends yet again on the dedication of one or two women in each area. The groups were started on a minute budget which covered little more than an initial mail shot. Most offer regular evening meetings with an invited speaker and some help themselves to become self-supporting by organising workshops and/or charging a token admission fee.

The Women and Training Group is one of the few women's networks that has full-time staff, currently based in Gloucestershire. They play a key role in the continuing work of the group and are a valuable source of information. They are able to provide information about training material which has been specifically developed for use with women. They have a list of valuable sources and can supply contacts of providers of training and will be able to furnish information on research that has been carried out in the last ten years which looks at various aspects of women's employment and training. It is fair to say that the group has been a major influence within industry and some companies have changed their operational practices following attendance at a workshop or conference organised by the group.

Much of the work carried out has been aimed specifically at women managers and the group has been criticised for the narrowness of its approach. The thinking behind the decision to target women managers initially was twofold. In the first place women were under-represented at middle management level and above and it was felt that any initiative which could assist their progress would be welcome. Secondly it was felt that women managers had a wider sphere of influence and could themselves initiate the progression of women further down in the hierarchy. Sadly these hopes are not always realised as many women are still prone to act as gate-keepers rather than the role models on whom the pioneers pinned their hopes.

The Pepperell Unit

One of the most influential groups has been the Pepperell Unit of the Industrial Society. The unit runs a wide variety of courses aimed at both women and their employers. Some of the courses are sponsored either by industry or the public sector; all are reasonably priced. The Pepperell Unit also carries out in-house consultancy work and will advise employers on all aspects of equal opportunities from the policy stage to implementation. Although much of the work of the unit is concerned with gender issues they have recently carried out a race campaign survey the results of which have been published. They are now developing training materials and case studies for use in this area of work.

The Pepperell Unit has a regional network and they are introducing programmes of training which are relevant to the needs of a particular area. They have carried out significant research work in the insurance industry, looking at the barriers to women's management development, and as a result of this work have developed a three-day residential management course for women managers working in that industry.

A significant amount of the Pepperell Unit's activities are carried out in the education field. They regularly run conferences for school children, students and undergraduates in addition to workshops for careers advisers and women in education.

Government funding

Because of the high numbers of unemployed at the end of the 1970s and the beginning of the 1980s, it was relatively easy to obtain government funding for training projects geared to the needs of women. There was also a good deal of scope for innovation and for helping women to advance in areas of work previously dominated by men. As the numbers of unemployed have fallen so have government funds. With the introduction of the Employment Training Initiative the accent has been on training which is more directly funded by employers or at least shared on a 50/50 basis between employers and government.

A limited amount of pump-priming money is still available but this is being directed towards the provision of courses which have been designed specifically to meet identified training needs within a given geographical area. The aim is to facilitate a closer communication between employers, local colleges and other providers of training. Some money is also available for research and more research is being funded by industry as skill shortages begin to make industrial life more difficult. The first port of call for anyone making enquiries about the provision of training, research papers available or computerised lists of training providers, should be the area office of the Training Agency. A full list is provided at the back of the book.

Management colleges

Most of the management colleges in the UK run courses specifically aimed at the management development needs of women. Ashridge, Cranfield, Henley and Brunel all have proven experience in this area. Women only courses were started because the take-up by women on management development courses was low. Many of the original courses focused on assertiveness training, career and life planning and helped the women who attended them to pull out their stronger points producing, by the end of the course, a personal marketing plan which helped the women who attended to sell themselves to organisations. It was found when research was carried out into the obstacles which inhibited the career progression of women that women were much more likely to focus on their weaknesses than their strengths. A man would look at a job description and say 'I have most of the qualifications and some of the experience; I can learn the rest as I go along'. Women on the other hand tended not to apply for jobs unless they felt that they had all the qualifications and experience necessary.

Distance learning

One of the gifts to women produced by the technological progress manifested in the 1980s has been distance learning. The Open University was the first custom-built institution to offer a distance-learning approach to training and development. Since then the growth in the production of distance-learning material has been quite phenomenal. Distance learning offers the ultimate in flexibility, recognising that individuals learn at different rates. Tutorial assistance is an essential part of all distance-learning packages but is a minimum part of the total programme. The Open College has now joined the Open University to capitalise on the demand for flexible training and both these organisations offer 'Women in Management' programmes. Each of the area offices of the Training Agency has a *Directory of Open Learning* which lists distance-learning programmes currently available. The directory is the size of one of the London telephone directories which will give the reader an indication of the amount of such material currently available.

There are also a number of open-learning resource centres opening up in local areas. One of the largest is ENTEK Training Services which is partly sponsored by the London Borough of Enfield but is run on a commercial basis. They are able to advise companies about suitable open-learning materials and supply packages from the complete range of open-learning resources available. These include: computer based training, audio cassette and text, text-based materials, e.g. workbooks, video, video and text, interactive video and multi-media. A catalogue containing full details of materials available can be supplied on request.

Independent consultants

There is a nucleus of consultants who have chosen to specialise in equal opportunity issues and they have, as individuals, been able to influence some of the major companies in the UK. One of the first in this field was Rennie Fritchie, an energetic woman who has developed her career as a single parent supporting two sons and an octagenarian grandmother, who lived with the family. Her tough beginnings make her a sympathetic listener to the problems which other career women encounter and she is able to convince organisations of the motivation and dedication of working women who also perform a balancing act between home and work commitments.

Roger Pauli, managing director of Stuart Crystal, freely acknowledges the help that Rennie Fritchie gave him in helping to develop the women within his company. Roger was a member of the advisory board for the Women and Work programme which was set up by Aston University; Rennie was a visiting tutor for the project. Together they undertook a project within Stuart Crystal which sought to improve the role of women within the company.

The Stuart Crystal experiment

Stuart Crystal is a private limited company which has been owned by members of Roger Pauli's family for six generations. Thirty-two of the forty shareholders are daughters of the family but, until recently, none of them had been involved in the running of the business. There are now three daughters actively involved in the Group, one of whom took over the chair in February 1989. A granddaughter is currently working with the company as a graduate trainee, although not from a business or management studies background. She is studying for a degree in agricultural marketing but, having worked for the family firm during her holidays, she has opted for a career in industry rather than agriculture.

Stuart Crystal has three main factories in the UK; additionally they have 26 in-store concessions, four glass and china shops and small companies in America and Canada. There are 12 members of the group board of whom 50 per cent are non-executive, three of the non-executive directors are women. The head and deputy head of the American company are both women; the sales director on the Stourbridge site is a women; the factory manager of the Scottish factory is a woman who started work with the company as a glass engraver; Roger Pauli maintains that between 15 and 20 per cent of all middle and senior managers are women but has deliberately avoided keeping statistics comparing female and male positions on the job hierarchy. The company, at the request of its women, has no Affirmative Action Programme. The women employees prefer to gain their promotion on merit alone rather than have the company make a point of promoting a set amount of women to each level of the hierarchy.

Another interesting point about Stuart Crystal is that they prefer not to take graduates from the management schools. Roger Pauli has done so in the past but 'bitter experience has taught him that the graduates in question have too much unlearning to do'. He feels that MBA graduates particularly come into the job with a heavy macho image and promote themselves as high achievers.

The company climate is one in which both women and men work together for themselves and the company and the preferred management style favours individuals who see themselves as organisers and facilitators but who do not feel constrained to be seen to be bossing other people around. Stuart Crystal does recruit graduates but prefers its graduate intake to come straight from university and to have a degree in classics or modern languages rather than in science or business studies.

Our question about how Roger Pauli started his programme of development for women managers received a totally unexpected and somewhat unorthodox reply. He told us that he has 'some fairly quaint beliefs based on the work of the Austrian philosopher Rudolf Steiner, particularly the idea that each of us has several incarnations both as women and men'. The inner being intrinsically has no sex and to Roger Pauli it makes sense to work towards attitudes which are sexually unbiased. When he thought about women in management he realised that the openings tended to favour women who were able to behave like men. Roger Pauli's ideal environment will be one where men discard their aggressive, point-scoring male attitudes and feel able to work in a softer, more feminine style, thereby making it easier for women to feel comfortable and able to work in this arena. He feels equally that women must learn to discard the exaggerated feminine traits which some adopt in order to achieve their aims; the simpering sex kitten will definitely not be welcome at Stuart Crystal!

Of course no explicit edicts are issued to this effect and the accent is on leading by example. Managers are encouraged to be less concerned with personal position and more with personal development. Employees tend to work in small groups and are given authority to take decisions within the group but they do not have the ultimate responsibility for a given project; that is shared by the group. All employees are encouraged to spot the talent in their particular area and extend to employees maximum scope. If, for example, the gardener is really interested in the kind of plants that s/he is tending the next phase would be to involve them in how the gardens were laid out and the kinds of plants to be purchased; ultimately in this environment that gardener would then have the responsibility for organisation and purchasing.

When it comes to talent spotting and the mentoring role there are one or two people within the organisation who derive great pleasure in seeing subordinates develop. Inevitably, however, the very nature of the organisation is based on a power structure with the top people always trying to stay on top or move further up. Such people see the structure first and people second.

Roger Pauli dislikes formal management structures but admits that the hierarchical structure seems to work in some departments. One of these is engineering which is characterised by a triangular shape; 'they (engineers) have an instinct which says they want to put it that way. Production and sales however is a long thin stream with people relating to other people on either side and a very thin level of control from above'. Most companies have a structure and place their employees very firmly within that structure but what really happens, Roger Pauli maintains, is that people organise themselves in the way that they feel comfortable and at the same time pretend to be organised in the way that the company would like them to be! Future skill shortages within the Stuart Crystal organisation are likely to be in the areas of engineering management and design. The company will train to meet these shortages; the only trained personnel who are recruited are in the computing field. Some employees are given day release to attend local colleges that offer appropriate training in technical skills. In the course of the last three years women have been encouraged to apply for management jobs and the only part of the plant prohibited to women is in the glass melting area. Because 30 per cent of the content of glass is lead oxide there is a danger of damage being caused to an unborn foetus during the first few days of pregnancy and protective legislation prohibits women from working in this area. If a women could demonstrate that she were unable to conceive the prohibition would be waived.

There is a formal appraisal system and both employers and managers are encouraged to make this a two-way exchange of information. Inevitably there are some managers who find this difficult. The company approach to changing attitudes is patience, the steady drip of water wearing away the stone rather than the drum banging, stick waving approach of less inspired organisations. Inevitably there are casualties in the management team as those who do not feel comfortable with this approach give up and leave.

We pursued the enquiry regarding two-way appraisal with Roger Pauli's secretary Marion Butler. She admitted that she did not formally appraise him but she frequently pulls him into the office from his preferred place on the shop floor. She books an appointment with him and requests that they tackle the correspondence and other routine jobs. Marion is one of the many women playing supportive roles within British industry.

Her efforts will never be formally recognised outside the organisation for which she works. We must stress that she loves her work, is regarded by the family as one of its members and has many roles and responsibilities. The relationship between the two of them is one of mutual respect, admiration and trust. Marion is secretary to the family trusts, organises dinners for customers, visitors and members of the government, has recently taken on responsibility for the canteen ('Mr Pauli said the canteen manageress has no one with whom she can discuss her problems, can she discuss them with you?'). Marion has also taken on the responsibility for special projects from time to time.

Stuart Crystal is not just a manufacturer of beautiful glass, it is also part of the tourism industry and plays host to members of the public who are taken on a tour of the factory and subsequently buy crystal in the shop which is now part of the site. A museum is one of the other attractions and Marion played a key role in organising this. Marion, for instance, knew that one of the tour guides was an ex-librarian and would be ideally suited to comb records and archives. The tour guide is now curator of the museum.

Marion also helped to organise the women's development course, working closely with Rennie Fritchie to arrange a mix of women ranging from cleaners to director level. She felt that the course was a 'great leveller' by enabling women at all levels to appreciate the problems faced by others. The course concentrated on confidence building, assertiveness training and using initiative and each course was over-subscribed.

This is an interesting partnership. Marion describes her boss as a man who has vision, who is rarely overwhelmed by the prospect of tackling something new. Marion tends to dismiss her own role which is frequently the 'doing' role whether she does it herself or selects someone to fill a position. Her willingness to shoulder responsibility is given full reign and her job has developed many facets because of this. She says that she feels trusted but never used and enjoys her job enormously. She is appreciated and trusted with her employers' cheque book and the keys to his home.

We wrote in a previous chapter about male dependency on women which is perhaps becoming eroded as more women seek employment, but persists equally in men who have always been cared for and who come to expect that the vision will be fulfilled through the hard work and devotion of others. Thus Marion, as a trusted secretary, has taken on some of the domestic responsibilities for the male directors of Stuart Crystal. Although these domestic tasks, taking shoes to be mended, clothes to be cleaned or sending birthday cards to nephews, are carried out during work time and not in her own time there is a tendency for men to use their secretaries as extensions to the caring network of women – wives, mothers, nannies, without whom, for some, life would be intolerable.

Developing the Euro-manager is already under way at Stuart Crystal. They are members of the European Managers Association and the equivalent organisation in Scandinavia as well as the European Glassware Institute. Much of the equipment needed for the manufacture of glass is bought in Europe and this helps to establish further trading links. The company also takes a small sales space at the Frankfurt Trade Fair. The German and English glass trade has been fairly well integrated over the past few years; the French have remained apart and may well continue to do so after 1992.

The work which has been started in this company for women will be on-going, particularly the assertiveness training. There is also an in-company network of women who hold regular meetings, normally attended by a nucleus of 12 women and from time-to-time the occasional male. This company is a good example of one where activity has been sparked off by external agencies, triggered into activity by a man of vision and put effectively into action by the dedication of one woman, in this case, the managing director's secretary.

Brighton Borough Council is an example of a local authority which has taken positive action to achieve equality of opportunity among its 2000 employees. They have publicised their policy statement both internally and externally and have used a number of different consultants to run courses for both women and men, all of which helps to reinforce the policy statement. All personnel who are involved in interviewing have to attend the equal opportunity programme to eliminate the possibility of unconscious discrimination at the interview stage. One of the writers of this book was employed originally to run assertiveness training programmes for women. As the word began to spread, following the initial two or three courses, a request came to run the same course for men. This challenge was quickly accepted and three men only courses were run; delegates ranged from scientific, engineering and sales staff employed at the well known Brighton Pavilion to the local dog warden! The men responded well and were open about their own particular hang-ups – apparently the feeling that the tradesmen are ripping you off is not limited to females! An interesting comment on these courses from other employees of the Borough was that women delegates were told they were going to learn to be aggressive, the men were told they were going on the wimps course! The original furore has now died away and mixed sex courses are run regularly with both sexes feeling comfortable in the company of the other. When assertiveness training was first introduced to the UK most of the early courses were run for women. The recommended reading list is an indication that this training was seen as a positive help for women. Men are increasingly admitting that their aggression can be tempered, an example of women only training adapting well to masculine use.

Although the role of outside agencies and consultants is often quite crucial when a company decides to take positive action to improve its equal opportunity programme, it cannot be stressed too much that the real work of implementation is ultimately the responsibility of every employee within that organisation. The role of the consulting agency is only realised when advice is turned into achievement.

6 Women Returners – the Career Break

The term 'women returners' is almost an innovation of the 1980's reflecting a changing attitude to the position of women in the workforce. It reinforces the view that women do not leave the workforce on a permanent basis when they have children but rather take a break for a period of time. The length of time taken for this break is continually being reduced by the combination of factors like smaller families and earlier returning to work. The average gap in employment has shrunk from 14 years to less than five over the last two decades. Ninety per cent of women who leave work for domestic reasons will return, mainly for economic reasons.

The employment situation for young men and women entering the workforce is rapidly becoming more equal with the number of female graduates rising and greater emphasis on women training in non-traditional female occupations. In some industries women score better than men with female graduates being seen as being more mature than their male counterparts. Marks and Spencer currently have an intake of 62 per cent female graduates for their management development programme and find their progress totally compatible with men's – until the baby break.

Most of the evidence of female employment patterns points to the fact that the career break for women has a completely disproportionate effect on their career prospects and individual development. There are two main reasons for this:

1. The enormous shortage of part-time jobs which either carry status or offer career progression. There are almost no part-time managerial jobs despite the high demand from women for these.
2. Individual loss of confidence becomes an acute problem for women who stay at home to care for young children. This causes women to lower their expectations of work and to undervalue their skills and experience.

Fifty-one per cent of women returners find work in a different occupational category from that held until childbirth. Of this number, 37 per cent return to work in an occupational category below that of their last job. The lack of child-care facilities and the fact that part-time jobs are concentrated in the lower occupational categories means women must forfeit the potential to utilise and develop their skills in order to work. This constitutes an enormous waste of talent for the nation where trained teachers are taking jobs as cleaners, nurses as canteen assistants and graduates as typists. For the employer who has invested time and money in training and developing women, it is a gross mismanagement of resources.

In looking at the position of women returners we must recognise that there are two categories of women in this position. First there are women who seek continuity of employment by taking maternity leave and then returning to the same company. Second, is the growing number of women who seek to establish a new career, perhaps in a totally different field, following the time spent away from work. Both categories have a great deal to offer employers in terms of experience, maturity and skills which have traditionally been undervalued whether by prejudice, inflexibility or oversight. Only now, with increasing economic pressures and labour shortages in key areas, are employers beginning to recognise that women returners present few problems that are insurmountable.

Weighing the costs

The benefits accrued from recognising the special needs of women returners far outweigh the losses forced upon both parties by rigid views on how work should be organised. For employers where women are a high proportion of the workforce these losses can be very damaging. Marks and Spencer, for example, found that 49 per cent of women on maternity leave did not choose to return to work. It was this unacceptable loss of human resources that caused them to rethink their strategy for women returners and to find ways of making it possible for women to combine family responsibilities with work commitments.

Taking a fresh approach

Marks and Spencer started with the issue of continuity and they looked at ways to encourage women to remain in contact with the company while at home and then offered a refresher course on their return. They also became one of the first companies to establish part-time managers within their stores. They currently have 48 female managers working part-time and two women job sharing. Although in these early stages of experimentation most of the women are working in personnel at the smaller stores, there are also two departmental managers and two administration managers. They recognise that their extended trading hours make it impossible to have any one manager on site during all open hours therefore it should not present major difficulties to become more flexible about when people work.

Building on the growing success of their returners policy Marks & Spencer are now implementing a more formalised policy which will be incorporated in their terms and conditions of employment. This includes the opportunity to take a break of up to five years and return to a job at the same status with all the benefits previously received. They are also now looking at the second category of returners, those who are currently seeking employment, as a valuable source of new recruits. In particular they are helping to develop employment opportunities for women by working closely with women returners' courses which are run for the benefit of women who, having taken a career break, now want to get back to work.

Women returners' courses

Public awareness of the notion of women returners has been raised by the special efforts of women's training organisations in particular. In the early stages a great deal of assistance was given by the MSC (now the Training Agency) who funded several workshops, the Women and Training newsletter and courses specifically for women. In 1981 a special workshop was held called 'Managing or removing the Career Break' under the auspices of the Training Division of the Training Agency. It was attended by representatives from Industrial Training Boards and other individuals who were active in the field of training for women. This workshop dealt with a variety of issues concerning the management of career breaks and was designed to promote new approaches by employers and individuals.

At the workshop it was noted from a preliminary survey of employers that many were prepared to be adaptable to help individuals cope. However, Margery Povall, Research Fellow at the City University Business School, made the point that whereas it was one step forward to see individuals being able to negotiate special arrangements, what has started as a special privilege 'can and should be converted into a right'. She went on to point out that 'Childbearing is a demanding and rewarding part of many people's lives . . . it is not sufficient reason to render half the population financially dependent on the other half either personally or through state benefits'.

Since 1981 there have been many other initiatives taken to help women who are seeking to bridge the career gap. Specialist organisations like Women & Training, the Pepperell Unit of the Industrial Society, the Women Returners Network (WRN), various colleges around the country and many independent women's trainers have run returners' courses for women. These courses are designed to deal with the special problems faced by women who feel they have lost contact with the business world and need skills and knowledge updating. The content of the courses generally tackles career/life planning issues and a typical programme may include building confidence, recognising strengths and weaknesses, finding support, planning ahead, setting goals and preparing action plans. They also include the more practical aspects involved in getting a job such as preparing a good CV, interviewing skills and a systematic approach to job search.

The Training Agency, with help from the EEC, sponsor Wider Opportunities for Women (WOW) courses which run over several weeks and encompass a broader view of opportunities at work and training in general. These courses usually include work experience placements and it is in this context that employers who offer placements recognise the potential to identify and recruit new staff. Like the YTS and employment training schemes it is worth the investment in supporting these programmes because they create opportunities for employers and employees to discover each other.

The women who attend these courses benefit in a variety of ways:

1. Their confidence is boosted through the support of counselling offered by both trainers and participants.
2. They begin to identify the likely paths they would like their career to follow
3. They begin to recognise the skills and experience they have already acquired and how they could be used to advantage in a job.
4. They learn how to plan and organise their career strategy by setting objectives and goals.
5. They develop interviewing skills and a positive approach to job applications.
6. They identify further training or courses that may enhance their career prospects.

7. They develop contacts and start to form a mutual support network.

In most cases women completing the courses will have a clearer idea of what they want to do and how to achieve it. They will look for employers who will be able to help them achieve their objectives with priority given to those companies which offer training and development opportunities.

One of the main facets of a women returners' course is the recognition that women who spend time rearing a family continue to develop skills and experience which can be transferred to the workplace. The organising skills required to run a household and rear children are in fact very closely related to management skills, like time management, negotiation, prioritising and taking responsibility for the development of others. It is often the language used for business skills that separates women from the job rather than the ability to do it. Textbook terms like leadership, motivation, decision making, planning and controlling carry powerful images which are alien to many women's terms of reference. These need to be translated into words which reflect the values of women who may well be used to 'planning and controlling' but recognise these same activities as organising and running; caring and enabling. These skills are not generally recognised by women as 'managerial' so it is therefore extremely helpful for them to be shown how to formally evaluate the job of a housewife/mother in terms normally used for organisational job analysis.

Women are often inclined to overlook other achievements made during a career break. Many women use this time to become involved in voluntary work which can bring invaluable work experience. It may have brought their first encounter with committee work or working in groups or teams. They may have taken special responsibility for some aspect of the voluntary organisation as treasurer, publicity officer or fund raiser. Some women discover they have good communication skills either as a contributor to a newsletter or by giving talks about the organisation to local groups. Any one of these skills could be a starting point for a new career and further demonstrates that a career break is not a time for standing still. Returners courses serve to raise awareness amongst women that they have more skills than they may realise to offer employers.

Adopting a positive view

From an employer's point of view there are some positive messages put forward by those who support women returners. If growing numbers of women are prepared to spend time and effort attending courses and workshops prior to returning to work they are clearly motivated to want their return to work to be a starting point for a new career rather than simply wanting a job. They do not see themselves as looking for pin money but rather as seeking job satisfaction with opportunities to develop as an individual. They will look to a company that is able to recognise this fact and provide scope for their talents. The pool of labour in the women returners' market is growing: of the 90,000 increase in the labour force predicted for 1995, 80 per cent will be women. This pool of labour is not bottomless, however, and those companies that offer the best opportunities will take the cream.

Companies can also learn from the training content of returners' courses. The natural process of confidence loss is just one of the reasons why women fail to apply for many of the higher grade jobs available. Offering bridging courses to update skills or retrain women provides a real incentive for women to tackle new areas, especially where there are acute skills shortages like computing or technicians. This retraining can include some of the most successful elements of career bridging courses such as assertiveness training or managing home and work. It has been shown that given the right support women very quickly restore lost confidence and adapt to a new working environment despite marked changes in management philosophy and in technology. In general there is a need for more employers to give active and financial support to returners' groups and courses which are at present inadequately funded but which can have such positive results.

Retaining skills and employee commitment

Although companies are increasingly looking to the open labour market for women returners they must first address themselves to the wastage that occurs from within by not adopting a retainer scheme. We have already seen the evidence of Marks & Spencer who, having adopted an informal scheme, are now expanding this and formalising the process. This is necessary because traditional employment practices make it impossible for most women to manage both career and family. Employment legislation on maternity leave is quite inadequate for most women to adjust to the demands of their new role at home. These facts, together with the high cost of skills wastage, are some of the main reasons why the EOC has reported a marked increase in the number of enquiries from employers who are contemplating the introduction of a career break scheme.

Career break schemes

Schemes to help women combine the responsibilities of family and work were la gely pioneered by the finance sector in the UK. The Returner Scheme, which was initiated as a research project in 1980 by the National Westminster Bank, has now become a part of its personnel policy and has been taken up by other banks. The project started by identifying 47 women who had recently left or were about to leave for domestic reasons. These women were interviewed to find out if they were interested in returning to the bank later. Their views were also sought on ways of keeping in touch during their absence.

This project has been well documented in the past. It is not generally appreciated, however, that the beginning was so modest. Nevertheless, the results have spread like ripples in a pond when a very small pebble is sent skimming across the surface. There were three major results following the initial project:

1. A retainer scheme was set up and was the first ever in the private sector in the UK. It was a significant innovative breakthrough in the employment of women and a symbolic recognition of the changing patterns of employment and the important contribution that women are able to make in the workplace given the appropriate encouragement and opportunity.
2. The project demonstrated the ease with which the women could be reintegrated into a familiar organisation after as many as ten years away. Retraining needs were in most cases minimal and their domestic lives were enhanced by the variety of experience and the new income.
3. The major result was that traditional management attitudes and, to a lesser extent, practices towards re-employing women were changed. Managers found that the re-employed women were excellent workers, although not all were dedicated to the pursuit of a high-powered career. Many managers began to keep lists of ex-employees who might be available for relief work or for regular part-time work.

Other benefits of the scheme were a reduction in recruitment and training costs through the return of mature, experienced workers with a known work history. Women who feel they will be welcomed back are much more likely to work at improving their skills in the hope of career progression. Continuity means that married women no longer feel that they are marking time until the inevitable process of starting a family will cut short their careers. The major benefit, however, is undoubtedly the competition which has now been engendered in the banking world as each seeks a way to encourage women to come back to work.

Following the success of the National Westminster Bank Returners Policy, three of the major clearing banks formally introduced a policy of allowing women to take a total break from work for between two and five years without loss of seniority.

Pat Sloane, Management Development Manager for the Midland Bank, has produced some of the most user-friendly recruitment literature designed to attract the enthusiastic and ambitious. Midland are one of the first employers to acknowledge that running a home and raising a family will have developed organisational and time management skills. They offer full-time, key-time and key-time auxiliary appointments. The latter are designed to appeal to employees who do not wish to commit themselves to a set number of hours each week. They are contacted during peak periods which could be a marketing launch for a new product or simply to cover for other staff who are on holiday. Midland have also opened two workplace nurseries and have plans to extend this number throughout the country.

Similar schemes are now being adopted by the engineering industry where skills are at a premium and women have the confidence to dictate their terms. It is interesting to note that in the banking industry this came about through the recognition that it was becoming difficult to recruit sufficient staff. It was therefore a corporate decision to implement equal opportunities policies and include a returners' scheme to reduce labour turnover. In banking women are in the majority whereas in engineering they are in the minority. In engineering companies it has more often been the case that highly qualified women engineers, faced with the constraints of limited maternity leave, have themselves asked for special arrangements to help them accommodate a break that has raised the issue. In some cases it has simply never happened before because there were no women. The Ove Arrup Partnership returners' initiative came about in precisely this way. Two women engineers suggested to the chairman that a formal returners' policy would be welcomed by female staff and he asked them to make suitable suggestions for a policy. They investigated good practice, made a report and the policy was accepted without question.

Good practice

The main aim of a career break policy must be to enable career minded women to combine a career and family. There must be a commitment to the view that this is desirable for both social and economic reasons:

1. Economic: To attract and retain high quality female skills.
To reduce loss of skills and investment in training.
2. Social
   To demonstrate full commitment to equality of
   (a) opportunity for women.
   (b) To minimise the problems faced by women having to make a
   difficult choice between work and family.

The starting point for the implementation of career break policies is in the generation of data relating to women in the organisation. Carole Truman in her research report 'Overcoming the Career Break – A Positive Approach' suggests the data needed would include:

1. Recruitment rates of men and women (past and projected)
2. Workforce analysis by age, grade, promotion rate and length of service.
3. Analysis of maternity leavers by grade and length of service.
4. Analysis of maternity returners by grade.
5. Analysis of investment in training and development of maternity leavers.
6. Analysis of costs of replacing maternity leavers.

'Once such data has been generated, organisations will be in a position to identify which policies will most effectively address the career break issue. Central to this will be consultation with staff in the organisation to discuss which initiatives will be most appropriate.'

Although each company wishing to implement a returners' scheme will need to assess the terms which serve their needs best, these will be tied to the best elements of good practice already established. Drawing from the experience of several companies these include guidelines on the length of break offered, terms for re-entry, contact maintained during the break, training and development offered and flexibility in employment hours where necessary.

Length of career break

The statutory provision for maternity leave entitles women to 40 weeks starting from the 11th week prior to confinement and up to 29 weeks afterwards. This applies to women who have been employed for two years full-time or five years part-time (8–16 hours a week). During this time they are entitled to six weeks maternity pay at nine-tenths of normal pay less the amount of national insurance maternity allowance. These years of service have to be completed by the beginning of the eleventh week before the expected week of confinement. If the woman wishes to return to work she must inform her employer in writing so that her job is kept open by temporary cover.

Although an increasing number of women are choosing to return to work within this period of time there are still many for whom it is not practical. It is more often the case that women find this period of time inadequate for their need to adjust to the demands of motherhood. For many women it can take the first year after the birth of a child (especially the first one) to regain the ability to relate to matters outside the home while managing the demands of a baby effectively. Not all babies fit into the 'textbook' model, feeding and sleeping at regular hours. Any new situation presents an element of stress and if this is combined with a lack of sleep and a demanding routine, it can present major difficulties for the mother. In these cases a longer period at home is necessary, but mothers would be more likely to be prepared to commit themselves to returning to their job if they knew that they had support from employers to do this. The time set for this break may be between two to five years depending on the circumstances, perhaps two for one child but five allowing for women who wish to have more than one child in succession. It has been found that in many cases women do not take a single career break but will return to work for a period of time before extending their families. Some companies may therefore prefer to offer a two-year break with the option to take a further break after say at least a full years's service on return from the first break.

Re-entry

The main element of a returners' policy is that women are able to return to work at the same status as when they started their break. Unlike the statutory requirements where a woman's job must be kept open during maternity leave, a returners' policy enables the employer to fill the gap left by the loss of an employee taking a career break. Many of the women who are restricted to the minimum maternity allowance may genuinely feel they would like to return to work and then find, when the time comes, they are not ready or able to return. Few parents are fully aware of the real impact and change of lifestyle a new member of the family can bring. Thus although the employer has kept the job open this effort is wasted by the loss of the employee. Planning for re-entry at a negotiated time which is more realistic not only increases the number of women willing and able to return to work but also enables employers to plan human resources more effectively and accurately. Marks and Spencer, for example, have found that those women who make a positive decision to take advantage of their retainer scheme do return to work.

Re-entry to the company may not be possible in the same job or even the same location. These issues should be discussed thoroughly with the employee before agreement is reached on the terms for re-entry and what is acceptable to both parties. This should also include factors like salary (usually at the same level as when ceasing to work with allowances made for inflation) also any training that may be necessary to bring the employee up to date. Although salary and employee benefits are not normally given to the employee during the break, continuity of employment may be one of the major benefits of encouraging women to return to the same company. In these terms her employment contract has not been terminated but merely suspended until she is free to continue her employment.

Maintaining contact

A vital element in any returners' scheme must be to keep the employee in regular contact with the company. By doing this the employee feels and is recognised as part of the organisation and retains some loyalty and interest in its current development. It also helps the employee to keep up to date with changes that inevitably occur and can provide a valuable resource of extra hands in times of emergency or short-term additional manpower needs. Some employees may be able and willing to work regularly, say at weekends or in the evenings to earn extra cash. Some companies make it part of the policy that employees should work at least two to four weeks a year during the break.

Other methods of contact include receiving regular mail from the company, invitations to meetings or conferences, opportunities for training and participation in company networks. Boots, for example, run a returners' network group which offers advice and support to those who are away from work, as well as those who have returned.

Flexible working

Flexible patterns of work are another by-product as companies begin to adapt their working patterns in order to accommodate women who have young families. On a daily basis a flexible day is broken into flexible and core or key periods. Traditional rules apply during the core or key periods; only during the flexible periods may employees arrive and leave according to their workload and private commitments. For the people involved the system offers an improvement in the quality of working life, the freedom to avoid rush-hour travelling and to adjust working time to accommodate workloads and family commitments.

The benefits to the company can be seen as a happier, more willing staff who can work more effectively because of the individual adjustments they are able to make. Employees also respond more favourably to being treated as the adults they are. A typical flexible working day is shown in Figure 7.

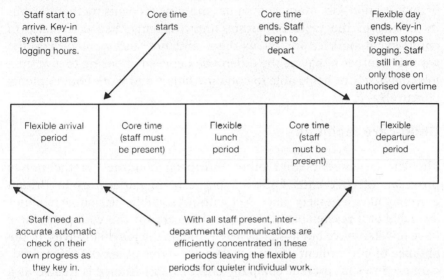

Figure 7 *An example of a typical working day*

Another popular and useful way to help women return to work is through job share which has been described as a unique and flexible way of filling full-time vacancies with the experience and versatility that two people with corresponding skills bring to a particular job. This theme is expanded more thoroughly in the next chapter along with further details of flexible working patterns. Although job sharing is particularly useful for the woman returner and can help ease her into full-time work, it can also be used for personnel who are approaching retirement age as a means of easing their passage from full-time employment to total retirement.

Any company wishing to implement a returner scheme must first accept that flexibility of approach and consideration for the returner have to be viewed along with the needs of the company. It is not enough to offer low paid part-time jobs in the hope that women with skills to offer will come flooding in through the front door. It is also unrealistic to think that an invitation to reapply for a job at a later stage will encourage women to reinvest their skills in the company without some additional incentive for them to do so.

Flexible working arrangements including flexitime, job sharing or part-time working are an important aspect of helping women to return to work. The various methods are described in detail in Chapter 7 demonstrating that there are enough options available for both employers' and employees' needs to be met in whatever type of organisation or job. Many companies are now recognising that flexibility is one of the most important improvements they can make in employment policies for all workers and not just women. For the women returner it may be the difference between choosing to give up a job completely or being able to combine family and work commitments effectively.

Child-care facilities

The UK lags well behind other European countries in the public provision of child-care. Only 1.3 per cent of under-fives in Britain currently have a nursery place. Yet without suitable alternative facilities available at a reasonable cost to provide care for the young, mothers have no alternative but to stay at home and do the job themselves. In the absence of government assistance, even in terms of tax relief for child-care expenses (at present company child-care assistance is treated as a perk and taxed as such), it must lie with the employer to decide whether it is feasible or economical to offer help with child-care provision.

For the employee the cost of full-time child-care can be prohibitive, an option only open to the highest paid, which is why so few women attempt to return to work full time. Malcolm Wicks, Director of the Family Policy Studies Centre, reported in *The Independent* that 68 per cent of under-fives with graduate heads of family gained child-care compared with 45 per cent of children whose family heads had no educational qualifications. He sees good quality child-care as not just an economic benefit enabling mothers to work but also as an essential social benefit in widening the experience and development of young children. Social deprivation often stems from the poverty of parents unable to work as well as lack of exposure to educational experience in the early vital years of learning. There are a variety of methods of child-care used by parents, from childminders to day nurseries each one offering a different dimension of experience for the child. Quality and choice are the factors uppermost in the minds of most parents but unless this is available cheaply (and in some cases freely) many employees will be denied this choice.

A survey published in the *Industrial Relations Review and Report* suggests that there is a surge of interest from employers who are considering the provision of workplace nurseries. Of the 32 organisations making use of workplace nurseries who were used for the survey, it was reported that not only does this improve retention of staff but that demand constantly exceeds supply. It has been predicted that the provision of child-care will become a core rather than a fringe benefit in the years to come with 50 per cent of usage being through male employees.

A survey of companies in the United States offering child-care facilities showed that the majority of employers reported that child-care programmes had positive effects on productivity. At Hoffman-La Roche in New Jersey, 78 per cent of parents surveyed said that their own performance had improved after the introduction of a child-care facility. Absenteeism had fallen while morale had risen.

The London and Manchester Group plc found that improved staff retention was one of their fringe benefits after incorporating a nursery into their new premises when they moved from London to Exeter. Their original aim was to demonstrate they were a 'caring company in practice' although the facility has now proved to be a valuable incentive for the recruitment of women. Andrew Burke, the Group's Personnel Manager reported at the IPM Conference in Harrogate, 1988 that although London and Manchester were fortunate in having a tailor-made site for a nursery which was purpose-built, 'you don't have to have 80 acres to start a nursery – it can be on a rooftop'. It is, however, important that the strict regulations laid down by Social Services are adhered to which includes factors like a staffing level of one adult to four children.

For most employers the provision of a full-time nursery would prove impractical because of numbers eligible, lack of space or the expense involved. However, it is quite possible to reserve places at a local nursery or crèche or to join with other local employers for a joint venture to overcome these problems. Most employers are reluctant to give an allowance towards child-care because it gives a greater benefit to some employees rather than others. Nevertheless, this should not be ruled out, especially where travelling to work deters women from using a workplace crèche facility. The cost may be far less than trying to provide in-house care and must also be weighed against the cost of recruiting and training new staff. The Institute of Personnel Management set the standard by stating that their philosophy is that an employer should be prepared to help their employees come to work. They pay 50 per cent of child-care costs up to a maximum of £20 per week to help their employees return to work. These and other similar initiatives serve not only to retain valued members of staff but also to demonstrate the companies' real commitment to equalising opportunities for women at work.

7 Changing Work Patterns: Towards Flexibility

The theme of flexibility has become a key issue in the 1980s and it is one in which women may be perceived to have a central role. Not only are women used to working flexibly when combining work with family matters but they also need and demand greater freedom to adjust working hours to make room for other commitments. This freedom can only be brought about by an acceptance of the advantages of flexibility and the practice of non-discrimination in the recognition of the contribution made by individuals to the organisation on a pro-rata rewards basis rather than part-time or full-time status.

'Flexibility is already here though we often don't realise it', wrote Mike Martin, manager for planning and recruitment for Texaco Ltd in an article for *Personnel Management*. He was referring to the search for the 'flexible firm' which is able to cope with rapid movement and developments within the market. The need for greater profitability and efficiency in the face of high employment costs is raising the profile of manpower planning in terms of creating a workforce that can readily adapt to demand. This is not simply a question of updating knowledge or learning new skills, it is also a process of creating flexibility in working patterns which allow greater fluidity of hours worked.

Flexible working times

Some of the ways in which this will be accomplished were identified in a report by the International Labour Organisation which suggested that 'the standard working week, mainstay of commerce and industry since the industrial revolution, may now be in permanent retreat'. This is being brought about by the increasing adoption of newer patterns of work such as:

1. Averaging hours over long periods, even on a yearly basis.

2. Introducing flexible rostering.
3. Varying the weekly rest day.
4. Tailoring work schedules to meet individual needs.
5. Staggering hours.
6. Compressing the working week.
7. Adopting other forms of flexible or part-time working.

The National Economic Development Office (NEDO) echoed these views in their survey published with the MSC: 'Changing Work Patterns – How Companies Achieve Flexibility to Meet New Needs'. The report shows how the increasing price of change and high unemployment have been major influences shaping the growth of part-time work and temporary employment. Changing work patterns since 1980 have also included the introduction of flexibility in working hours and new shift systems; multiskilling and team working, pay flexibility and subcontracting. These can be split into four main categories: numerical, functional, pay and distancing.

A report, 'Labour Flexibility in Britain: the 1984 ACAS Survey', suggests that some forms of flexibility previously associated with the service sector are now being widely adopted in manufacturing industries. The increase in the use of part-time workers was particularly notable along with the introduction of shift working. These two aspects go hand in hand demonstrating that it is quite possible for one worker to take over where another has left off. This ensures better use of capital investment in technology and machinery helping to increase output and decrease overall costs. The ACAS survey showed that the manufacturing industry was hardest hit by recession and that flexibility had been introduced primarily to reduce labour costs, meet fluctuations in demand and increase competitiveness.

The examples of increased flexibility within companies demonstrated by these surveys and many other case studies now being published show that traditional notions of work patterns are undergoing a transformation. In West Germany the concept of flexible working has been extended further and some companies now base their human resource demands around a flexible year. Under this system employees contract to work a set number of hours each year and are then more or less free to work them when they wish. These schemes also make economic sense in a business economy where most references are annual and fluctuations can be evened out over a broader reference period.

The Beck-Feldmeier experiment

The largest of the West German firms to have introduced flexible working is the department store Beck-Feldmeier KG, which has about 900 employees. Before implementing the flexi-year the company conducted an attitude survey to discover how many full-time staff would be interested in working shorter hours. They discovered that 38 per cent of full-time staff wanted to work fewer hours and additionally 21 per cent of part-time staff were interested in working less.

Beck-Feldmeier were also concerned at the mismatch between the availability of salespeople and the number of customers needing attention at various times of the day and from season to season. There are daily peaks and troughs in the retail business, as in most others, and staff were not always available at peak times. Some of the time employees would be standing around with nothing to do, conversely at other times there would be queues of customers waiting to be served. The dual role of the company therefore was to improve productivity at the same time giving the workforce more freedom over the times they worked.

As a first step the company allowed a considerable number of employees to change to part-time work over a period of a year. The effect of this step was that the original division of labour into 65 per cent full-time and 35 per cent part-time has now been reversed. The company also began to study when people were really needed in each of its departments, only then did the company feel ready to introduce its flexible working year scheme.

Under the scheme employees can choose, at six-monthly intervals, the number of hours they want to work over the next year. Full-timers work 173 hours a month. Part-timers can choose between 60 hours and 160 hours per month, in increments of 10 hours. The most popular choice is 110 hours. Personnel planning has been devolved to the individual departments; employees are provided, via the supervisor, with the data about when people are needed. Small groups of employees decide among themselves when and how long they work. The supervisor arbitrates as liberally as possible, trying to co-ordinate the interests of the company and those of the employees.

Each employee is free in principle to work three months on and three months off; to work only Mondays, Wednesdays and Fridays or to work any arrangement that suits their particular circumstances best. A typical arrangement might be that an employee who has chosen to work an average of 110 hours per month would work 150 hours in January, when the children are at school and when the company needs extra help to cope with the January sales. In February she may work 70 hours and take a skiing holiday. In March she could work 173 hours in order to build up a credit which will enable her to accompany her husband on a business trip abroad. This also helps the company during a busy spring period when customers are buying new clothes.

Whatever the hours worked during the month, the salary cheque remains the same. During the holiday season, when business is slow, employees tend to accumulate a lot of their debit hours which they then make up during the busy period of November and December. The time control thus operates like a bank account which is sometimes in credit and at others in debit.

The company finds that employees generally are very conscientious about maintaining a healthy balance. The biggest deficit so far has been 50 hours. If a particular employee consistently has difficulty in meeting their agreed number of hours the company renegotiates with them. The company is able to make a fairly accurate prediction of how many people will be needed in each department each day, and at each hour of the day and the employees try to fit in with these requirements. A certain amount of over or undermanning is however inevitable.

In order to resolve this problem, the personnel department places on a computer all the data concerning departmental manning needs and employees' preferred times of working over the period. It then arranges for spare employee time in one department to be allocated to another department which may have a manning deficiency.

Normally in retailing companies people do not like to move from one department to another on a temporary basis. Beck-Feldmeier have overcome this problem by charging the cost of the personnel loans to the receiving department, so it pays the supervisor with excess sales-people to loan them out. The employees accept the temporary transfer, which may be only for two hours, as a necessary concession in order to make the flexi-year system work.

Since the company started the scheme they have been able to tap into a vast pool of part-time labour and this has upgraded the quality of the sales employees. The company finds that because they offer interesting work arrangements they get interesting people applying for jobs including women in the 35 age group who have been bringing up a family. They are generally well educated and do not want, or need, to work full-time. Although the cost of training this group of recruits is high there have been substantial savings in recruitment costs and sales per employee hour have increased, showing that employees work harder when they are employed at the time during which they want to work. Absenteeism and labour turnover has fallen and the company no longer needs to advertise for job vacancies – employees come to them. The supervisory staff took longer than their subordinates to adapt to the new system; with experience however they have learned how to use their personnel in more cost effective ways.

The impact of competition, recessions, revival, new technology and social change have bitten into the hard-edged view that work is a 40-hour, 40-year process for individuals. The above example of flexi-year working demonstrates a scheme that can be adapted to meet the needs of other organisations where there are peaks and troughs of productivity, while making it easier to cover for staff holidays and sickness.

Later entry into the workforce, early retirement, shorter working hours, redundancies and skills shortages have all made their contribution to changes in manpower planning. The personnel function is learning to manage these changes by reviewing recruitment and assessment procedures, pay policies, terms and conditions of employment and training. British Telecom have now introduced apprenticeship training to the older worker (40 or more). A new Holiday Inns Hotel, recently opened in Swindon, has recruited all its staff on the basis of multiskilling and flexible hours, setting a pattern which will gradually be introduced to other hotels in the chain.

It is now possible to adopt an open mind about the number of hours and the way in which people contribute to an organisation. This should be based on rewards for the contribution made by individuals rather than restrictive job categories and narrow definitions of part-time and full-time work. Flexibility is brought about by removing the divisions that restrict rather than develop employees.

Part-time work

During the 1970s when recession was hitting hard, full-time jobs were reduced yet at the same time over a million part-time jobs were created which represented an increase of 34 per cent. Ninety per cent of these jobs were for women with nearly half of all female employees working part-time. Industries like Hotel and Catering employ part-time females as almost half their total labour force. Moving into the 1980s this trend has continued, helped by a general improvement in the economic outlook. In the period 1986–1987, 257,000 additional workers were employed in the labour force, 110,000 of these vacancies were filled by women working part-time. The ratio of one in five part-time workers is likely to be revised to one in four in the 1990s demonstrating a significant change in overall working patterns. These figures confirm the view that employment trends are moving away from full-time male jobs to part-time female jobs.

On the surface it may appear that this major increase in jobs for women has improved their employment prospects. It has in the sense that more women have been able to obtain work but, so far, little has been achieved in removing both formal and informal discrimination against part-time workers. As Beechey & Perkins point out:

> Part-time jobs are highly segregated from full-time jobs, especially from full-time men's jobs. It is extremely rare to find a woman working part-time doing the same job as a man. In the main, part-time jobs are manual jobs in service industries and occupations and they are usually located at the bottom of the occupational ladder. Even those women who work part-time in higher-level jobs – in administration, for example, or nursing, teaching and social work professions – are almost always in the lowest grades.

Apart from working on lower grades with lower pay, part-time workers are usually excluded from benefits such as sick pay, maternity pay, paid holidays, overtime pay and occupational pension schemes. It has been estimated that 62 per cent of Britain's part-timers are excluded from most of the employment benefits afforded to full-time workers. Britain has the highest rate of employment for female part-time workers in Europe and yet it has one of the worst records for payment and benefits.

A report on women and employment (Martin and Roberts, 1984) points out that:

> Part of this problem arises from the view that jobs which carry responsibility cannot be done effectively by people who are absent for part of the time. It is also the result of a historically moulded perspective that full-time jobs are the domain of breadwinners and careerists whilst part-time jobs serve to supplement family incomes. The fringe benefits of full-time work were not seen as relevant or necessary to part-time workers who already have a 'breadwinner' in the family. In addition employers cite the high cost of employment as a reason for not extending benefits to part-time workers, especially where non-contributory pensions are in operation for full timers.

These arguments serve only to perpetuate discrimination building a demarcation line against the flexibility that is necessary for change.

Defining part-time work

Strictly speaking part-time workers can be defined as anyone working less than the normal full working week. The Government sets guidelines by using the definition of anyone whose normal basic weekly hours are 30 or less for its 'New Earnings Survey'. Thirty hours are also considered full-time by the DHSS and supplementary benefit is refused at this level; families on low pay must apply for a Family Income Supplement. Part-timers working less than 16 hours a week are not covered by employment protection laws (unless they work at least eight hours a week for five years for the same employer). This is in itself discriminatory; if we look for example at all local government manual staff where 34 per cent are women working less than 16 hours a week. Helen Hague, Labour Reporter for *The Independent* noted that:

> The National Union for Public Employees is one of the few unions to have reduced subscription rates for part-timers. It has now framed a 10 point charter directed at Government and employers to give the part-time workforce parity with its full-time colleagues on holidays, sick pay, bonus schemes, maternity pay and pensions.

She quoted Rodney Bickerstaffe, NUPE's general secretary as saying:

> Part-time workers make up nearly a quarter of Britain's working population, but their role in the workplace and beyond is relegated to second division status. It is high time we broke the bonds of their invisibility and battled for the decent deal part-timers more than deserve from the Government, employers and the trade union movement.
>
> Our aim should be to ensure that part-time work is a genuine choice for all employees, rather than the only option open to women with responsibility for the care of children or elderly relatives.

Clearly all the evidence points to the fact that the employment of women on a part-time basis presents one of the greatest contributory factors to inequality at work. Both government and employers need to review policies regarding the contributions and benefits afforded to workers which will bridge the gap between the two categories of full-time and part-time. For example, National Insurance contributions may be paid on a pro-rata basis and with transferable pension schemes optional for all employees which have built-in flexibility to be raised or lowered according to current needs.

For women with children the number of hours worked may be minimal while the family is very young but may be gradually increased as the children get older. Removing the leap from part-time to full-time work helps to ease employees into a more demanding role with greater confidence and less disruption to the family. This kind of flexibility can benefit employers by providing a framework for fluctuations in demand. Working time can be increased or decreased by negotiation according to both the needs of the employee and the company.

The number of part-time jobs has increased very largely because employers need more women to work for them and offering shorter hours is one of the best ways to attract women to the labour force. Most of the women who work part-time are married and choose to work less hours because they have other responsibilities. They also find other benefits which add to their job satisfaction like travelling at 'off peak' times or having added relief to monotonous jobs. However, as we have noted earlier in the book there is a very significant number of women who are employed well below their qualifications or capability levels. These women have compromised their situation because they choose part-time hours not because they prefer more menial work. Their skills and experience are redundant simply because they are unable to conform to a standard working pattern. This pattern has been set by tradition rather than a rationale that is appropriate to the technological revolution. John Atkinson, research fellow at the Institute of Manpower Studies told delegates at a conference held by the Industrial Participation Association that 'Companies were not just turning to part-time workers because of the scarcity of labour supply. Service sector employers were recognising the advantages of older female employees in terms of customer service and reliability'.

He posed a number of questions which he felt should be on the agenda of human resource managers in the 1990s:

1. How far up in the hierarchy in terms of status can a part-timer go?
2. How real are the constraints which keep the vast majority of part-timers at the bottom of the pile?
3. Are remuneration and benefits packages flexible enough to allow the integration of part-time and full-time jobs and the growing movement between the two?
4. How should legislative provision adapt to provide a basis for employment standards?

Reviewing part-time options

Standard part-time jobs that give reasonable rewards may be ideal for situations where only limited hours are necessary to complete the job, but there are other forms of work that require different solutions. For many jobs longer hours are necessary to complete the work though this does not automatically mean that this must be the task of one person. Shift systems are used in most industries and these can be adapted to meet the needs of both employers and employee preferences. Martin used the example of a company producing jute which introduced a five-shift system to replace the traditional continental four-hour shift. The change was in response to union demands for a shorter working week, from 42 hours a week to 39 hours a week. The new system increased the number of shifts from 213 to 226 to be worked, spread more evenly over the year by reducing the number of plant closures for public holidays from four to just one over Christmas. The reduction in hours was compensated for by the creation of 120 new jobs but at the same time overtime has been significantly reduced by 50 per cent. The impetus for change here was the demand for increased leisure time but clearly systems for increasing the number of shifts can be used for further reductions in working time to accommodate part-timers without reducing pay levels.

Voluntary reduction time

Increased leisure time can be introduced by the simple method of giving employees the choice to reduce the number of hours they work. Experiments in America have demonstrated the popularity of introducing the option for full-time employees to exchange salary for additional time off. The system became established in San Mateo, California under the title 'Voluntary Reduced Work Hours (V-time) Programme' in 1977 and by 1982 it was made permanent. Employees can choose an annual percentage of time off which can then be allocated as shorter working days, shorter working weeks or in blocks of annual leave.

A similar scheme was successfully established in the State of New York which allowed employees to reduce work schedules by a minimum of 5 per cent and in further 5 per cent increments upwards. Started in 1984 the programme had almost 1000 people enrolling within the first 14 months. The option to reduce hours worked by 10 per cent meant that employees could take one day off a fortnight which can be invaluable for women with children who need to occasionally attend school, do extra shopping or care for a sick child. In effect the employee is almost working full-time and in many cases probably does a full-time job yet at the same time has the confidence of knowing that whenever necessary they are entitled to take time-off. For the local authorities who introduced the scheme it was seen as a very effective way to reduce costs.

'New Ways to Work – San Francisco' published a resource manual *V-time: a New Way to Work* which outlines a typical V-time programme:

1. Reductions of work time (and pay), ranging from 2.5 per cent to 5 per cent, 10 per cent, 20 per cent, and 50 per cent are offered.
2. The schedule remains in force for a designated period usually six or twelve months, to allow employees and employer to try out the new scheduling arrangement, with the assurance that the commitment can be either renegotiated or terminated at the end of that period.
3. All employee benefits are maintained; some are pro-rated.
4. A supervisor must authorise an employee's participation in the programme.
5. The time off can be taken either on a regular basis, as a reduced day or week, or in a block of time, such as extra vacation or days off work.

'Depending on the programme, an employee could have almost limitless possibilities for balancing work with other responsibilities such as family or school, gaining new skills, responding to an injury or health problem, or phasing retirement.'

Pam Walton of New Ways to Work in London reported that:

> According to a survey carried out by the European Commission in 1985, one in six full-time employed workers in Europe have a very keen interest in a significant reduction in working hours, even if this is associated with a corresponding loss of pay. Ideally they would wish to work approximately 30 hours a week, rather than the conventional half-time employment. The survey found that actual working hours and desirable working hours do not coincide for almost half the workers in Europe – and that there is considerable potential for new forms of part-time work among persons at present in full-time employment. One in six employees would, if they had the choice like to work to a yearly number of working hours.

Pam Walton feels that V-time has enormous potential within the UK, especially for the large numbers of people who would like to reduce their working hours by a small percentage rather than by half. However, the response to implementing similar programmes to the Americans in the UK has so far been slow, despite the availability of information 'New Ways to Work' carry in their office. At present most of the interest in flexible working patterns seems to be focused on job-sharing schemes although V-time may be one of the major patterns for the future.

Job sharing

The attraction of job sharing for employers is that they get two workers for the price of one while for employees they gain all the benefits of full-time employment on a shared basis while working part-time. Unlike work sharing, where jobs are split by reducing the volume of work to create more part-time work, job sharing enables employees to undertake all the responsibilities of a full-time job by volunteering to share the position. As long as each person is working at least 16 hours a week in any week that they work, the terms and conditions of employment can be shared pro rata according to circumstances.

In the majority of cases employees tend to apply jointly for a shared full-time job although it is possible for the job to be split in two, especially where very little interaction is needed by the partners. This may involve a split week or working alternative weeks or even alternative days. In these cases employers may advertise for two part-timers either to fill a full-time vacancy or one part-time worker to work with an existing employee who can only work part-time.

Many job sharers prefer to work more closely together creating additional flexibility by covering for each other during sickness, holidays and time off. In these cases demarcations of responsibility may be drawn on the basis of suitability for different areas of work according to experience, preferences and personality. (It is even possible for job sharers to be rated at separate incremental points for different levels of experience.) Integrated sharing can work especially well in jobs with heavy commitments and responsibilities; the work can be balanced more easily. When pressure is at its highest both parties can be at work, one say attending a meeting while the other deals with a pressing issue that needs full-time attention. The additional time worked can be compensated for by time off at a later stage when pressures are removed.

Most of the attention on job sharing has been focused on white-collar jobs especially in Local Authorities and the service industries. However, as the Equal Opportunities Commission note in their handbook: *Job-sharing: Improving the Quality and Availability of Part-time Work*:

'there is no reason why job-sharing should not be adopted in manual employment too.' The booklet summarises the benefits job holders may negotiate to share on a pro-rata basis:

1. *Pay* Sharers are to receive the same rate as full-time workers and are to be paid pro rata according to the number of hours worked.

2. *Holidays* Sharers are to have pro rata the number of paid days holiday as full-time workers. Bank holidays are to be divided between sharers according to the number of hours worked.

3. *Sick pay* Sharers are to be included in the sick pay scheme on the same basis as full-time workers, and receive sick pay on a pro-rata basis. Sharers are not to have State Sickness Benefit deducted if they are not receiving such benefit.

4. *Pensions* Sharers are to be included in the pension scheme on the same basis as full-timers and paid pro rata their highest earnings over 20 years.

5. *Maternity/paternity* Sharers are to be included in the scheme on the same basis as full-timers, but receive maternity/paternity pay on a pro rata basis

6. *Training* Sharers are to be included in all training schemes and opportunities, and are to have equal access to training facilities. Job sharers may take it in turns to attend training courses.

7. *Promotion* Pairs of job sharers are to be considered for promotion in the same way as full-time employees.

8. *Increments* Sharers are to be placed on the appropriate incremental 'point' for their experience, but paid pro rata. Individuals who share jobs may, depending on age and experience, be placed on different incremental points.

9. *Overtime* Where sharers work beyond their normal hours but not outside the normal working day, they are to be paid for the extra time on normal rates or to take time off in lieu. Sharers are to be paid overtime rates only where they work beyond the full-time working day or where they work unsocial hours.

10. *Car allowances* Where a lump sum car allowance is payable the allowance is to be divided between the sharers. Where a mileage allowance is payable, each sharer is to receive the allowance in the normal way, i.e. according to mileage travelled.

The EOC's survey on job sharers showed that on balance the advantages of job-sharing outweighed the disadvantages. The employment costs for job sharers are only very marginally higher and can be balanced by positive factors like a reduction in turnover, increased efficiency due to greater flexibility, more continuity and higher energy levels from sharers. They also point out the advantages of attracting a wider range of candidates from the employment pool, especially talented women who are not available for full-time work. Employing two such women offers a much wider range of skills and experience than is possible from one person.

Some initial doubts were expressed about the practicality of employing managers and supervisors in a job-share situation which may cause confusion amongst subordinates. However, if standard procedures are adopted and agreement reached on management styles and practices this should present no difficulties. There will always be employees who try to use the difference as an excuse for poor performance. The situation can be compared with parental responsibility in the sense that one partner is played off against another. It is more often an advantage to employees to have a shared boss in that some individuals relate to one better than another. This can improve employee relations by allowing subordinates to discuss problems with the partner with whom they feel most at ease.

For the job sharers themselves, it seems that the major disadvantage to this form of part-time work is that there is a tendency to work longer hours than officially recognised. This is very common with many part-time jobs but for sharers it is exacerbated by the constant need to communicate on joint issues. A great deal of this is done in at least one person's time off and very often in both partners' own time. However, this disadvantage is offset by the benefits of having a partner with whom to discuss work issues. This can help ease problem situations considerably and is known to be a more creative and motivating way to work. There can be a considerable balancing effect in working with another person who counteracts any negative feelings on bad days and adds a fresh surge of energy when necessary.

Although there are no accurate statistics on the number of people actively involved in job-sharing schemes there is evidence that this number is continually growing. A survey of job sharing in local authorities carried out by New Ways to Work in 1987 found 56 authorities with formal job-share policies employing over 2000 job sharers. The number of vacancies advertised for job sharers is noticeably increasing and these can be added to the applications made by job sharers for full-time jobs where the employer is persuaded to accept sharers. Much of this interest can be attributed to the need for women to find a more equitable way of working part time, thus avoiding most of the drawbacks attributed to part-time jobs. Indeed, it is now being demonstrated that some of the most responsible jobs can be successfully shared including general managers, Fleet Street editors, Stock Exchange executives, hospital consultants, researchers, in fact almost any worker.

Teleworking

One of the most recent developments in the introduction of flexible working patterns is the use of teleworking by companies. Rising costs, the expansion of the communications industry and the increase in technology, together with a greater desire on the part of individuals to manage their own work, have fuelled the drive to adopt this technique of employment. The advent of electronic mail, facsimile machines, computer processing, electronic filing and the instantaneous ability to transmit information anywhere in the world have opened up the possibility of working patterns which were once the creations of imaginative science fiction writers.

Teleworking is still in its infancy with most experiments in the UK taking place through computer companies where the right equipment is readily available. One of the most famous examples of its potential for success has been the computer systems company 'F International' which was set up 25 years ago to allow computer professionals to combine work with caring for children. Their system is built on using a combination of freelance workers and salaried full and part-time workers working mainly from home and using this as a base for visiting clients. Contact between employees is maintained by meetings with supervisors both locally and at head office, otherwise leaving employees the flexibility to work within the hours that suit them best.

This new development in homeworking provides the option for employees to work wholly or partly at home using new technology to establish a 'home workstation'. Not only does it provide the employee with the facility to use flexible hours and reduce travelling time and cost but it can be a major cost-cutting factor for employers. Rank Xerox, for example, found that a third of their costs in running their business were tied up in buildings, electricity, service costs, security and maintenance. They embarked on a 'networking' experiment to help reduce these costs by selecting suitable employees to establish home offices and carry out project work for the company.

Contact with the company is maintained by invitations to meetings and a neighbourhood office was established in Milton Keynes providing a base for six homeworkers. The services provided by outworkers are not confined to computer specialists, they also include market research, tax advisers, business planners and personnel consultants.

Although in some cases the increased use of homeworkers has been a cost-cutting exercise, it is also used by others as a means of retaining experienced workers or expanding the workforce. ICL, for example, were anxious not to lose the services of female employees and developed a system of freelance homeworking for female programmers who had decided to start families. This was later changed to give home-workers employee status providing holiday and sickness benefits pro rata to the number of hours worked. These arrangements have the built-in advantage of providing greater flexibility of hours worked to accommodate fluctuations in the demand for labour.

The move towards telecommuting is by no means widespread at present although the Henley Centre for Forecasting predicted that it is likely to become much more common in the next ten years. Although it is not suitable for jobs which require regular face-to-face contact with others like receptionists there are many jobs which have defined or measurable objectives like bookkeeping or clerical work. There are others, like salespeople or researchers, where regular changes of location are part of the job and these can be co-ordinated from a home office base. It is often a case of determining whether the individual is suited to working from home rather than the constraints of the job. Rank Xerox have found it necessary to use personality tests and interviews to discover the individual needs for affiliation or team working. There is usually a greater need for time planning and self-motivation to organise working schedules at home and the support of the family is paramount in ensuring success.

In structuring the pattern for allowing employees to work from home Richard Upton, writing for *Personnel Management*, suggested companies must also consider the following points:

1. Changes to working practices of a homeworker's colleagues and

superiors (including need for appropriate controls and communication channels).
2. Direct and indirect costs to be borne by the company.
3. Is the proposed remote working location suitable and safe?

It may also be necessary to implement special training for managers and supervisors of homeworkers to ensure quality and output controls are tight enough and communication is carried out effectively.

The status of teleworkers is also a matter for serious consideration by companies. Although many home-based workers may prefer to consider themselves self-employed for tax purposes this may not be acceptable where the employer maintains a high degree of control over the work done. If there is a mutual obligation to provide and perform work then the tax authorities may regard this as employee status and impose National Insurance and PAYE contributions, backdated if necessary.

'Teleworking is not futuristic but is alive and well. The new mastery over time and geography may lead to some of us adopting a pre-industrial work pattern – and staying rather than going to work.' This was the conclusion of a conference on 'Tomorrow's Workplace' organised by the Confederation of British Industry and British Telecom. It is certainly seen by many as another important aspect of the new 'flexifirm' adding a further tier of manpower resources to the central base of 'core' workers.

This view is echoed by the report in *Industrial Relations Review and Report* journal following an analysis of teleworking in two large private sector organisations and one local authority. The survey shows that teleworking eases recruitment and retention problems by:

1. Giving employers a vital extra element of flexibility in employment strategies.
2. Tending to raise the individual's productivity.
3. Demonstrating its popularity: one company had far more applicants than jobs available and further research has indicated up to a quarter of all employees were interested in teleworking.
4. Expanding the recruitment pool by opening up new opportunities for working parents and disabled workers.
5. Gaining support for the unions.

The report also highlights some of the positive aspects of current teleworking practice. Whereas originally all teleworking staff were women, 50 per cent of applicants are now men. Pay and employment benefits are rated at an equivalent status as employees corresponding with overall high ratings on staff appraisals of teleworkers. Most teleworkers maintain regular contact with the office through meetings and correspondence thus avoiding the possibility of isolation or losing contact. Finally it is increasingly being recognised that teleworking can be applied to a wide range of jobs; the local authority concerned estimates that up to 500 job categories could be considered for this form of employment.

The positive results shown from the variety of forms of flexible working currently being practised are an indication of how this trend may continue. Nevertheless, as Anna Pollert of Warwick University's Industrial Relations Research Unit argues in her discussion paper: 'The Flexible Firm: a model in search of a practice' we must beware that this is not merely the expansion of 'an insecure, casual, poorly trained and cheap employment "periphery" which is the last thing needed to improve Britain's productivity record and competitiveness'. These categories may well describe much of the work done by women at present but they have no place in our future.

8 What Kind of Training Do Women Need?

Success for women is no different than for men. To do well in a job, women must have all the basic training that is necessary for men. The only difference there appears to be between men and women is that women seem to get less of the type of training that helps them to progress beyond the unskilled and lower levels of employment. They are prone to becoming trapped in occupations that become blocked at prescribed levels like secretaries, clerks, nurses or assistants. Career progression is limited by lower expectations on behalf of both employer and employee. The problem is further exacerbated by the difficulties of social and organisational barriers which only the most determined, career-minded women seem able to resolve by working harder and better than most men. These problems can only be resolved by adopting a more positive attitude to women's participation and development within the workforce by using training as one of the main tools of support.

Special initiatives may be necessary to market training to women including single-sex training where necessary to help overcome attitudinal barriers to self-development. This is especially appropriate in persuading women to consider the non-traditional areas of women's work. British Telecom, for example, produces a special publicity leaflet on Technical Opportunities for Girls showing women at work in overalls and safety helmets. The leaflet outlines their training opportunities to become technical trainees using women employees as role models for career opportunities. The Engineering Industry Training Board, supported by the Training Agency, offered grants to companies to contribute towards the cost of training women to become technicians.

The printing industry has also been a traditional male domain which has been seen largely as the result of custom and practice rather than a deliberate intention to discriminate. In order to break into the cycle, in 1984 the MSC funded a major project named 'Women in the Work-place' which aimed to:

1. Encourage employers to offer training to their women employees in order to increase the pool of skills and talents available.
2. Encourage women to take up training in order to improve their employment opportunities.
3. Provide training designed specifically to meet the needs of the women themselves, their companies and the industry as a whole.

Part of the project has included grants to employers for women's training with many companies reporting positive results from the outcomes for both employer and employee. Reports on their successes were presented at a conference held in 1985 where Liz Bargh of the Pepperell Unit pointed out, 'The way forward now is not only to give women training but also to begin to train men and women to work together'.

These kinds of initiatives demonstrate the importance of raising the profile of women's training to make it acceptable to both employers and individual women. Training at all levels is necessary to bridge the gap between women and men at work, from basic skills training to management development. We have already discussed the limitations of employers who view women as a secondary workforce concerned only with supplementing a family income and with limited ambitions. Given support and encouragement most women would increase their skills and develop their interest in work to the same levels as men. This process begins with ensuring that women's training needs are accurately assessed and opportunities are presented to help them move into more challenging areas of work. Accurate assessment may well include recognising that some training may need to be specially designed to help women overcome confidence barriers to raise their awareness of what they can actually do.

Many employers are beginning to recognise their responsibility to give particular attention to training for women in order to ensure greater equality occurs. The Women and Training Group report in their ten-year review that increasing numbers of employers are turning to them for advice and information on how to develop special training initiatives for women. One of their responses was to organise a two-day workshop in November 1982, 'A Practitioners Workshop on Training Materials for Women'. Twenty leading practitioners in Britain, working in the area of women and training, were invited to share experiences and pool resources. Subsequently, these and other suggestions for women's training activities were published in the *Women, Work and Training Manual* which contains almost 100 exercises for use in women's training workshops. Many of the exercises contained within this manual relate to basic workskills like managing meetings, speaking in public or improving interviewing skills. One of the major issues addressed is career/life planning which forms the basis for all other forms of self-development along with assertiveness training and confidence building. These skills are clearly an essential starting point for women's training because they deal with areas known to cause the initial blocks for women's progress at work. Not only do they help women overcome blocks but they also create a more positive attitude within women on their power to achieve more at work.

Basic skills

The strongest basis for career development is gaining breadth of experience through which employees are able to understand their strengths and weaknesses. Part of the process of career planning is to discover what you are capable of doing well and what you feel you could develop further by training, education and work experience. This concept is built into graduate training schemes which are planned to incorporate limited exposure to a broad range of activities. This is done on the one hand to help trainees gain a wide perspective and understanding of the company's operations and on the other to enable them to learn about themselves and what areas they may choose or be able to develop further. Traditionally such mobility has been limited to young people selected for their potential to progress rapidly within a company. Other employees are usually hired for a specific job and given the necessary training to stay with that job until such time as they are selected for promotion or choose to leave. Mobility has rarely been seen as suitable for other categories of workers who may also potentially benefit from exposure to other departments and types of work. Now, with the current emphasis on multiskilling to improve efficiency and increase flexibility, it is possible to offer all employees the chance to broaden their experience within an organisation. Holiday Inns have formally adopted this practice and recognise that it offers an opportunity to identify employees who have the ability to increase their responsibility. Since women are so often concentrated in jobs which offer little or no progress it is important to consider methods in which their experience and training can be extended. The ways in which this can be done varies enormously according to the size and nature of the company in which they operate. However, the principles involved are closely related to the concept of continuous development which is becoming more generally recognised by trainers as an important aspect of combining learning and job satisfaction for most employees.

The Institute of Personnel Management *Code of Continuous Development for People and Work* defines continuous development as 'self-directed, lifelong learning' which is brought about by company policies 'first to allow and then facilitate such learning at work, through work itself'. The concept of continuous development gains acceptance by the recognition that each employee should be able to create some personal development plan. Benefits to the company accrue from planning to combine individual development requirements with the aims of corporate plans which anticipate the manpower needs for the future. This is particularly appropriate where new technology, expansions or change in general is programmed into the future of the company.

As part of the training process, continuous development follows the two basic stages of staff training: induction and skills training. Assuming that the women working within the organisation are performing effectively in their current jobs, the task is then to identify what measures can be taken to increase their potential to learn from their jobs and widen their opportunities. Mumford suggests that 'people can become self-directed learners, understanding their learning styles and developing skills needed for effective learning. Thus they can manage their own learning process instead of relying on the system, or hoping they will learn naturally'.

From this basis women can be helped in the process of self-development by the promotion of self-directed learning which will enable them to broaden their own horizons. To do this they should be helped to understand their own learning style and their personal responsibility for development. The company should assist in this process by ensuring that positive support is offered by getting managers and supervisors involved in taking a counselling role in developing personal development plans. This must be backed by training facilities which are readily available for learner involvement, whether formally (courses, workshops, projects) or informally (books, manuals, videos, access to experts). It is important that possible organisational barriers such as work routines, personnel procedures, access and assistance are examined and, if necessary removed. (It is also essential that appraisals are seen as part of the overall process of giving positive assistance to personal development plans.)

The theme of continuous development is dealt with quite comprehensively in Rosemary Harrison's book *Training and Development* where the key characteristics of a 'continuous development' team are summarised as:

1. All members, management and non-management, appear to understand and share ownership of operational goals.
2. Immediate objectives exist and are understood by all.
3. New developments are promoted: change is constructive and welcomed and enjoyed, not forced and resisted.
4. Managers are frequently to be heard discussing learning methods with their subordinates and colleagues.
5. Managers frequently ask subordinates what they have learned recently.
6. Time is found by all the team to work on individual members' problems.
7. Reference documents (manuals, specification sheets and the like) are available to all without difficulty, and are used.
8. Members use other members as resources.
9. Members do not just swap information; they tackle problems and create opportunities.
10. All members share responsibility for success or failure; they are not dependent upon one or more leaders.
11. Members appear to learn while they work, and to enjoy both.

These principles of training have particular relevance to the development of women at work because they promote a self-awareness which is often lacking in women's understanding of their potential at work. Following a continuous development programme helps women to discover greater strengths and a sense of direction. The onus on the employer is to provide opportunities to accommodate this individual growth that takes place, rather than offer compensatory training for women.

Specialist training needs

The process of self-development for women is actively encouraged by participation in specialist courses. A wide range of workshops have now been developed which have proved very successful in helping women to develop personal effectiveness and progress within their careers. Some of the most popular of these are described below, although variations and new courses are constantly being added to the list as women's career development gains greater priority in the field of employment. Most of these courses can be run in-house; some of the most innovative ones have been created by company training managers or equal opportunities officers themselves, like the training officer who thought of using an excerpt from the film 'Tootsie' on an awareness raising course for men and women. However, there is a wealth of training specialists available throughout the country, either working with colleges or networks as well as independent consultants specialising in women's training. A list of agents is given at the end of the volume.

Career/life planning

This course gained ground particularly with women returners as mentioned in Chapter 6. It has special value in the early process of raising awareness amongst women of the potential to create greater career opportunities. Above all it is a way of motivating women to extend their horizons by encouraging them to expand their vision through making better use of planning and organisation in their lives. Exercises in self-awareness help women to assess their personal abilities and recognise the skills and experience they have accumulated, again helping them to build confidence in themselves. These exercises then lead on to projections for the future and ways of furthering development. Individual goals are set and objectives planned in order to decide on the first steps to be taken. Action plans are prepared to ensure these objectives are met. Ideally, follow-up sessions are held at a later stage – say in four to six months, to review progress.

Companies may choose career/life planning workshops as a starting point for training groups of women who are employed in stereotyped roles like secretaries or clerks. It is often within these groups that women stagnate and have restricted horizons. The cost to the employer in these circumstances may be lack of motivation, high staff turnover and a wastage of talent. Clearly no employer will wish to encourage women to pursue goals by leaving the organisation, so this exercise must encompass visions of ways in which to develop within the company. This, naturally, means ensuring wider opportunities are genuinely available and encouraged for movement through training and promotion.

Gender awareness

This course is often treated as a precondition to the implementation of an equal opportunities policy. Its basic aim is to help people to understand the conscious and subconscious process at work in our perception of sexual differences. We have all been conditioned from birth onwards to make assumptions about people based on what we know, what we are taught and what we have experienced. Our early role model for a woman is usually our mother and we will naturally base many of our ideas about women on this model, however accurate or inaccurate. Although our views may be modified as we progress through life, most people continue to typecast, especially by gender, and carry notions based on stereotypes of the differences between men and women as we described in a previous chapter.

Gender awareness courses usually start with opening up discussion about what it means to be a man or a woman. Invariably when participants are asked to define the differences between the sexes a list of stereotyped views will be produced (see previous chapter). Discussion can then centre around how realistic these labels are and whether there are in fact greater differences in types and characters within the sexes than between them. Very often there are participants who refuse to acknowledge they see or treat the sexes differently and who express difficulty in defining the differences. However, if they are asked to look around them at what women and men are doing generally, in offices, on the train, within the family, on television etc., they are forced to accept that differences in role do occur and that this has some influence on their characteristics.

The purpose of gender awareness courses is not simply to expose different role perceptions but also to challenge the validity of these views and to look for ways of eradicating this bias. For women it can be a process of removing self-limitations and for men a recognition of their responsibility to treat women as equals. A successful conclusion is one that helps participants to treat individuals on their merit, for what they do rather than what they are. The exercise is helpful in dealing not just with gender bias but also racial discrimination and ageism which works against both men and women, white or black alike. Training can be a remarkably effective way of removing prejudice by challenging the bases for unfair treatment of employees.

Assertiveness training

Although assertiveness training has been found to be an excellent method of helping women to develop, it is by no means limited to women only. The skills of assertiveness are just as beneficial to both sexes as a means of improving effectiveness in dealing with people. Men can experience as many difficulties as women in expressing their feelings in a reasonable way, although often for different reasons. Men may accuse women of bursting into tears whenever things go wrong whereas women often accuse men of having no feelings. Both need to learn the art of keeping feelings under control so that they can be expressed positively and situations handled reasonably.

The basis for assertiveness training is to understand the rights of the individual; to be treated as a person who is worth listening to and who is capable of listening to others. As with life-skills training, this process begins with understanding oneself in terms of one's needs and wants as well as one's tolerances and limitations. With this understanding individuals can then learn, through role-play exercises, to handle stressful situations in a different manner. The sort of problems that are exposed during this type of training are difficulties in dealing with an unsupportive boss, a sexist colleague, an aggressive customer or a task-orientated supervisor. Trainees are seeking to develop the confidence to state their views without resorting to frustration or feeling powerless.

The benefits to the company in implementing assertiveness pro-grammes can be widespread, not the least of which is helping employees to feel more confident about their position within the company. Apart from motivating women to improve their circumstances this sort of training can improve customer relations and relationships between colleagues as well as managers and subordinates. If employees have a greater ability to express themselves, then problems can be resolved more readily and general feedback on how well operations are running will be more forthcoming.

Men and women working together

An interesting and more recent development in the field of specialist training for women's career development have been courses for men and women working together. Much of the development work has been done by the Pepperell Unit who have run a range of courses on this theme. They have stressed the importance of starting from the top with this course involving the most senior managers of organisations who are the policy makers and opinion leaders. These are the leaders who are able to create an environment for co-operation between the sexes.

The issues tackled by these workshops relate to two main themes: first, to challenge the view that careers must necessarily be based on the traditional male model and second, that men and women have complementary skills which are essential for effective teamwork.

Part of the awareness raising intended on this type of course is to open out views on how responsibility for home and family should be divided. The notion that domestic as well as work matters can and should be shared more equitably is an important factor, not just in helping women to succeed but in offering men a more balanced lifestyle. Using this theme further workshops have been developed on the subject of 'Divided Loyalties' to examine these issues in more depth.

Influencing skills

The capacity to influence is seen as one of the major routes to power and is therefore an essential skill for the development of women. Part of women's lack of self-confidence stems from their inability to sell themselves and persuade people. Ashridge College based their programme: 'Influencing Strategies and Skills' on research which highlights the areas of need for personal power:

1. The importance of influence in managing horizontal relationships with peers (research indicates that British middle and top managers spend between 47–66 per cent of their time with peers).
2. The need for well-developed influencing skills in specialist roles.
3. The particular need for women in the above situations who may also be working in a male-orientated climate.

Ashridge's programme was designed to help individual managers understand the process of influencing and developing strategies appropriate to their individual work situations.

There appears to be very little evidence that women in supervisory or management positions use different influencing skills from men. However, the widespread evidence of women's lack of influence in organisations demonstrates the need for this type of training to take priority in an equal opportunities programme.

Management development

Although women clearly need greater encouragement to apply for management training, the range of skills needed is no different from those needed by men to do the job. Priority should therefore be given to ensuring the number of female participants on management training courses is increased to achieve balance. This process includes removing some of the less obvious organisational barriers which may operate against women. A typical example of the kind of situation which can occur was demonstrated by the Banking, Insurance and Finance Union (BIFU) when carrying out an audit of staff at a company of major financiers. Few women were trained by the organisation for their sales force from which branch managers were selected. The result was that no women at all appeared on training courses for branch managers. It is clearly necessary therefore for greater numbers of women to be encouraged into the sales force or for branch manager selection procedures to be broadened out to incorporate candidates from other areas.

The traditional routes to management are often one of the main barriers to women's upward mobility. Opportunities may be curtailed by the career break or restricted by choice of occupation especially where departments lack prestige or status. One way to overcome this problem is to implement an accelerated development programme for women managers. Women who demonstrate potential may be selected for special training which is designed to rapidly increase the skills, knowledge and experience necessary for management. Programmes of this nature may be designed to cover a one to two-year period of intensive focus on the art and practice of management. They usually combine off the job training in specialist skills with on the job training to enable these skills to be applied to work.

AMI Health Care plc recently implemented a new programme for executive development which demonstrates the success of this type of initiative. Candidates are selected on the basis of application and interviews from a wide range of departments and roles. The programme takes place over a period of two years in which participants attend workshops, undertake a reading programme and tackle special project work. An important part of the process is the appointment of a mentor who works with the trainee to guide and help progress. The first year's result led to the promotion of eight of the twelve candidates demonstrating the effectiveness in creating an outlet for talent.

Accelerated development programmes have special benefit to companies in demonstrating their desire to recognise and cultivate employees with potential. They are a motivational tool for those who seek advancement and can build confidence in those who are reluctant to recognise their own management potential. Simply being selected and taking part in such a programme raises the profile of the candidate within the organisation and enhances opportunities for development. A programme for accelerated management development for women managers in the hotel and catering industry began by using one of its main long-term objectives: 'To assist women managers to become competent and committed members of the workforce and to gain their acceptance by employers as such'. This was necessary because it is so often the attitudes of employers that create a barrier to expectations of what women can or wish to achieve.

Many programmes start with career/life planning and assertiveness training helping individuals to take a positive role in self-development from the very beginning. If the promotion opportunities are available for those who succeed then the company gains from positions of responsibility being filled by enthusiastic, experienced and committed company employees.

Single-sex training for women managers

There are many, including women, who would say that it is not necessary to have single-sex training. The protagonists would argue that not only does it have very little benefit but that it is in fact unrealistic to train separately for work that is shared by both sexes. However, the MSC report *Women Managers: Their Problems and What Can Be Done to Help Them* highlights that only 22 per cent of the women they surveyed were absolutely against 'female only' training courses of any kind. The majority felt that single-sex training would have special benefits, especially for women at the early stages of management development.

The sample used in this survey comprised 696 female managers who replied to questionnaires sent to 1500 organisations from the major industrial categories. From the responses given, women managers suggested the types of training they feel is needed. These included:

Type of training	*Percentage of total sample*
Confidence building	50
Assertion	42
Interpersonal skills	12
General management skills including delegation, disciplining, negotiating	10
Learning to cope with men, including sex-role stereotyping, imposition	8
Political awareness	7

Training for men to cope with women   6
Desocialisation re: sex stereotyping   5
Leadership   5
Retraining women for entering workforce   3
Personal presentation   3
Power of speech and public speaking   3
Resilience   2
How to do well at interviews   2

Although interpersonal skills training may be perceived as necessary for both sexes in early management development, for women this need seems to persist at more senior levels. This may be due to their increasing isolation at the upper levels where women have identified difficulties in being taken seriously as a woman and in dealing with men. The same survey asked women what training skills they would like to develop with the following results:

Senior managers
    Managing people generally
    How to deal with men at work more successfully
    Putting over a less superficial attitude   people often don't know if I mean what I say
    Keeping up with new technology
    Consulting skills
    Skim reading

Middle managers
    Dealing with difficult staff, especially men
    Assertion skills
    Delegation
    How to be taken more seriously being a woman
    Disciplining

Junior managers
    Coping with being labelled 'the boss'
    Assertion and confidence
    Delegation
    Training abilities and assertion
    Managing more people
    Supervisors
    Finance and budgeting

Economics
Administration
More technical training
More mechanical training

The report concluded that 'the majority of women in junior and middle management positions still feel undervalued and discriminated against because of their sex' and that the results of their survey 'would tend to support single-sex management training for women managers, especially at junior management level when emphasis could be made on assertion/confidence skills training'.

The benefits of single-sex training begin with the special encouragement it offers as an incentive to train as managers. Ashridge College, for example, noted that over a period of years the female attendance on management courses sponsored by companies was minimal. When they set up their own 'Women in Management' course they found that they were inundated with enquiries, mainly from women applying independently. The desire from women themselves to have training is plainly evident though obviously not matched by employers' willingness to endorse the process with the same fervour. However, the fact that women responded so readily to a single-sex course indicates that they appear to be user friendly in a variety of ways:

1. Women only courses can be constructed to address issues that relate specifically to problems women encounter without fear of prejudice.
2. Sensitive issues may be discussed in a safe environment particularly where personal issues are concerned.
3. Women who find difficulties with sexism or male aggression can speak openly of events or circumstances which they find intimidating.
4. External courses offer the opportunity for women from different companies to explore issues common to all. Courses can be arranged to meet domestic requirements more readily.
5. In-house courses may encourage a wider field of employees' attendance from different departments.
6. Women only courses demonstrate an employer's positive commitment to equality of opportunity.
7. Networking contacts can be developed more readily between women.

Most of the single-sex training that is offered to women in management relates to confidence building and assertiveness training. The most recent development in this area has been in outdoor training which also incorporates the skills of team building. As with standard management training programmes it was noted that less than one third of employees who elected to take part on courses were women.

Two centres in particular, Outward Bound Eskdale and Outward Bound Rhownar in mid-Wales, have combated this problem by offering women-only courses. What they found was that the majority of women enrolling on these courses did so on their own initiative and paid their own fees. These were women who were prepared to meet a wide variety of challenges, including abseiling, rock climbing, canoeing and navigation. The aim is to test the individual's capabilities and gain insight into how people react and how they cope with these reactions.

Eden Carruthers of the Outward Bound Trust pointed out that, 'Women rarely have the freedom to test their own methods and therefore the women's course allows women to experiment and gain confidence in asserting themselves.' He added, 'Outward bound coaxes much hidden latent potential out of women and enables them to develop often underutilized resources'. A testing but relevant way to help women progress, outdoor training has also a multiplicity of gains for companies including:

Leadership training
Team development
Improving communications
Encouraging creativity
Coping with stress
Developing managerial and organisational skills
Improving interpersonal skills
Time management
Personal growth and assessment
Developing awareness of learning styles
Developing appropriate attitudes to risk
Re-energising

If these benefits are combined with the findings of the director of the Outward Bound Trust that women are 'much more receptive to group work than men and are definitely an asset to a course' there is every reason why more women should be considered for this type of training.

Self-development for women managers

So far we have looked at the ways in which training can act as an external agent to developing women managers but perhaps the most useful method has been overlooked. Companies can do a great deal to encourage women to develop; they can be selected and groomed for better things but the real process of development comes from within. Women can manage their own learning, especially where they find traditional management courses inappropriate. Self-managed learning provides a flexible structure for the individual to determine their own learning needs and style of learning at a pace they can handle. This process ensures that the outcomes of learning are related entirely to the individual and the situations that concern them. This method is best accomplished by working with a self-development group with the guidance by a trainer.

A project of this nature was initiated by a group of experienced trainers: Tom Boydell of Sheffield City Polytechnic, Rennie Fritchie, formerly of Transform and Valerie Hammond of Ashridge Management College. They define a self-development group as:

1. One that meets regularly.
2. Focuses subject matter on real issues at work.
3. Participants set their own aims and goals.
4. Issues are chosen by the participants themselves.
5. Methods used to work on chosen aims are selected by the participants.

The methods used are designed to meet the needs of the various participants individually and are generally unstructured. They may include:

1. Discussions of real issues to do with work, personal aspects of the self and of real issues to do with other aspects of life other than work or within the group.
2. Exercises and unstructured activities.
3. Lectures and formal inputs.

The MSC sponsored a series of self-development groups to be run for women in a variety of industries in order to evaluate their effectiveness in helping women to direct their own learning. The outcomes were judged to be very positive with most of the participants rating them very highly as a development experience. The benefits included increased confidence, the ability to be more assertive, thinking more logically, being less reliant on others for approval, being able to take on more responsibility, increased understanding and empathy with subordinates.

A very high proportion of women's training has been focused on women's management development. This has been necessary because there has been such an obvious imbalance of opportunities for women. An early hope was that, as the sphere of influence for women managers was wider than that of their subordinates, that good management practices would be passed on from woman to woman. In this area more than any other women can make their greatest contribution to industry and the cause of equality. Only when women have the power to set policies and make changes will industry achieve balance and be able to utilise its manpower resources to the fullest.

At least 50 per cent of the best brain-power in the UK lies within the female form, much of it waiting to be discovered and developed to the benefits of all. Despite ten years of Women and Training, backed by many excellent organisations, only 18.8 per cent of managers and supervisors are women and 8.3 per cent in senior or general management. There is still a lot of training to be done.

9 Mentoring

Mentoring is perhaps the single most economical method of management development available in today's organisation. Why? Because the mentors are already part of the middle and senior management structure. By definition they have a wealth of experience of the job and a comprehensive knowledge of the company culture which can be passed on during regular periods which are set aside for communication with the protégé.

Career development programmes which are designed only around the employee can stimulate morale, help employees to identify their own skills, set career goals and develop action plans to pursue those goals. These programmes do a good job in that they encourage self-reliance and initiative and help the employee to build networks with peers, at the same time as making their needs visible in the organisation. The problem, however, is that they frequently fall short of moving employees to the point of 'making things happen'.

When managers are trained to be effective career developers they learn to coach, appraise, advise and act as referral agents for employees. This assistance and support helps employees to check their own assessment of their skills and, at the same time, to learn more about their organisation. Employees are also given advice on selecting career goals and are offered training and development to help them to reach those goals. Not all managers fill this role adequately, sometimes due to lack of skill, more often due to lack of commitment.

Career development programmes which encourage the participation of higher levels of management can increase the payoff by the addition of the mentoring dimension. In the 1990s the accent for organisations will be the retention of skilled staff, because the demographic changes alone will make the acquisition of replacements a painful, long-winded and expensive process. It is generally easier for a mentor to find a protégé than vice versa. In theory any individual can approach a potential mentor for advice, in practice many are inhibited from doing so simply by the position occupied by the mentor in the hierarchy.

The *Oxford Dictionary* defines a mentor as 'an experienced and trusted adviser'; effective mentors play a variety of roles which help the protégé in the advancement and management of her/his career. If the relationship is effective it can last way beyond the time limits which are usually set in formal mentoring programmes and the mentor is later identified as one of the key influencers in the career development of the protégé. Before we look in detail at the requirements of a mentoring programme let us look at the various roles which a mentor is required to fill.

Sponsor

The primary role of mentors is to give guidance to the protégé and to help them to widen their exposure within the organisation and thus to build informal networks. A key role is to create opportunities for the protégés to prove themselves and thus demonstrate what they have to offer. These mentors may propose their protégés for membership of special project teams, help them with a project or to analyse a problem. They may coach the protégé in the presentation of ideas to higher levels of management and thereby give them increased visibility and the opportunity to shine. Mentors therefore can really make things happen which would normally be beyond the scope of the protégé's sphere of influence to accomplish unaided.

Teacher

Mentors as teachers can solve real problems and additionally create learning opportunities by offering hypothetical problems for the protégé to solve. Some mentors hold brainstorming sessions during which they listen to and guide their protégés in dissecting a problem and generating alternative solutions. Others bring their protégés into real work situations and then pose the question 'what would you do?' The protégé then begins to see the need for a continuous learning environment and the importance of getting as much information as possible and looking at several alternatives before finally solving the problem.

One of the most important aspects of the mentor's teaching role is to identify and pass on the organisational culture. Because most cultures contain both written and unwritten rules, the mentor can help to decode and transmit the key elements. Sticking to the unwritten rules is vital if protégés are to gain the acceptance of senior managers. They will never attain positions of power in the organisation without this acceptance. An excellent performance on its own does not ensure either mobility or success. The informal political culture is likely to embrace such subjects as dress code, company image, predominant management style, methods of resolving conflicts, the characteristics required of the 'outstanding' managers and what are the crucial values of the company. The mentor can share their own perceptions, give the protégé feedback on how they perform and present themselves and invite them, as observers, to high level meetings. They can tour several operational units and share their observations on how the organisational culture operates in each. An astute protégé can test her/his assumptions about the main norms of the system and pick up a good deal of additional information by listening carefully to how the mentor talks and to whom.

This kind of insight into the organisational culture is critical in the overall management of a career. Contentment and pride stem from being in concert with the values and beliefs of the company. If there is a severe mismatch the employee will become dissatisfied and her/his career will reach a plateau. Advice and feedback from the mentor can help to create a better fit and help the organisation to retain its highly valued employees.

Devil's advocate

When adopting this role the mentor challenges and confronts the protégé providing her/him with the opportunity to assert ideas and influence the listener. This is a particularly helpful role, all protégés need to learn how to maintain their power and influence with people much higher in the organisation. They discover a variety of ways of getting their ideas accepted, the mentor offers advice on what works and what does not. This helps to build self-confidence.

Coach

All mentors need to be supportive coaches helping the protégé to discover what is important to them, what skills they have, their interests and aspirations. A skilful mentor will create an open, candid atmosphere which leads the protégé to self-assessment and the discovery of what really counts for them. This can be facilitated if the mentor uses disclosing behaviour, sharing their own career histories, struggles and decisions in order to support the protégé in doing the same.

Mentoring programmes fulfil a variety of corporate needs. Most importantly, as we have just explored, they foster the growth of relationships between junior and senior managers. In addition they become a major component of the management development function and a formal mentoring programme will extend the system to groups who find it most difficult to gain sponsorship, namely women and ethnic minorities. Mentoring programmes can be a key factor in helping companies achieve their equal opportunities programme.

Implementing a mentoring programme

Careful planning is an essential first step and initially it will be a task for the personnel department who will outline the programme goals, the criteria for participation and the preferred method for mentor/protégé interaction. They will draw up a document which will make the goals and procedures explicit and this will be distributed to all the participants at the beginning of the programme.

Different companies will have different goals; in some it may be the mechanism for senior managers to communicate the corporate culture and values to younger managers; in others it may be a way of getting a senior manager involved with the training and development of a junior. It can be an excellent tool to ensure that women are not left behind in the management development race. Before the programme is implemented there are other factors which must be considered.

Who should participate?

This is a crucial question. Many programmes choose the mentors from middle management and usually from the same department or speciality as the protégé. Middle managers are probably best suited to help the protégé with job training. If, however, the programme aims to communicate the corporate culture a senior manager with a broader knowledge of the organisation's values and practices might be a better choice. Companies vary widely in their selection criteria for the protégé. Some organisations require all incoming junior managers to enter the programme, others will allow them to decide for themselves. It is the task of the personnel department to communicate the information about the programme to all newly recruited managers.

Matching the mentor and protégé

If there are departmental or speciality departments the choice of mentor may be limited as not all middle managers will be selected to participate in the scheme. Other organisations may allow the junior manager to choose from a pool of participants. The junior manager will interview the various senior managers to discover who could most effectively serve as coach or teacher. In many instances a process of natural selection occurs where a protégé identifies a senior manager s/he admires and respects. Whichever way is chosen the roles should be clearly defined in order that the expectations of the protégé do not exceed the ability of the mentor to deliver.

Length and timing of the programme

The length of the formal programme will depend on its goals. It is obviously useful if the mentoring programme runs hand-in-hand with the more formal aspects of the management development programmes within the company. In some cases six months is felt to be an adequate length, other organisations feel that a two-year programme is necessary if all the goals are to be met. The timing is a crucial factor. If companies are able to limit the recruiting of junior managers to a once yearly intake it will be possible for all new managers to start and finish the mentoring programme at the same time. If recruiting is staggered this will clearly not be possible, the programme will, however, be more difficult to manage. The programme can be evaluated more easily if all mentor relationships begin at the same time and group participation, for example involvement in senior meetings will obviously be easier to arrange if all participants are at the same stage of the programme.

Method and frequency of communication

All programmes vary in terms of the amount of interaction between mentor and protégé. A minimum contact has been established as twice a month for formal meetings but informal meetings can take place as often as practicable and desirable. If no formal targets are set for meetings the relationship can cease to be profitable for the protégé. The best place to meet is the mentor's office. This gives the protégé the opportunity to watch the mentor at work, to meet her/his colleagues and to get a feel for the working life and environment of a senior manager.

Mentor Responsibilities

The mentor must be adequately briefed about her/his responsibilities and given appropriate guidance on the achievement of the goals of the programme. Some companies regard a well-trained manager as one who is familiar with resources, departments and corporate practices. One of the key responsibilities in this case would be to introduce the protégé to the heads of various departments and to explain where each department stands in the overall corporate strategy. One company defines management training as an 'assimilation of new managers into the company and into an understanding of its culture and management styles'. Mentors are therefore asked specifically to discuss the particulars of corporate culture, including the importance placed on the company sponsored dinner dance. S/he explains to the junior manager the diverse preferences and management styles in use within the company and shares the unwritten codes and value systems.

Cross-gender mentoring

Because of the shortage of female senior managers it is inevitable that some junior women managers will have a male mentor. This could give rise to speculation, and accompanying office gossip, that the relationship is more than a purely business association. A study of the mentoring of young females was carried out by Donald D. Bowen, Professor of Management at the University of Tulsa, in which a total of 32 pairs was studied. All the protégés were female, 18 of the mentors were male and 14 female. They were drawn from a wide range of fields which included banking, insurance, personnel, health care, law, religion, accounting, television, retailing and politics. There was a similar wide range of organisational levels involved. The mentors ranged from first line supervision to president and from trainee to president or owner for protégés.

Each of the female protégés considered her relationship with her mentor to be an important career element; the relationship was also considered to be an important aspect of the overall career development. Protégés with a female mentor identified slightly more with them than did those with male mentors, the statistical evidence, however, was not significantly different. Free responses include remarks like 'my mentor is a person that I try to live up to' and 'my mentor is a person I admire immensely'. Protégé responses to the interview question 'What would you say is the most important thing you get from your mentor?' were coded in line with an analysis developed by Kathy Kram (Kathy Kram researched the mentoring process for her doctoral thesis in 1980 at Yale University. Her unpublished work is entitled 'Mentoring Processes at Work: Development Relationships in Managerial Careers'). Kram has identified two categories of functions which mentors perform for protégés. The first, which she describes as 'Career functions' includes sponsoring, coaching and providing exposure, visibility, protection and challenging working assignments. The second set of functions are labelled 'psychosocial functions' and require a more intimate and intense relationship. The mentor becomes a friend and counsellor as well as a source of competence, identity and managerial effectiveness. Kram further believes that role modelling is a psychosocial function.

Contrary to the expectations of the researchers the more intense psychosocial mentoring occurred where identification with the mentor was lower (mean = 10.3 *vs* 10.8 for the career function pairs). The psychosocial functions were more likely when the mentor was male (72.7 per cent *vs* 57.1 per cent for the female mentored pairs). Although these results were not felt to be statistically significant they oppose predictions based on the assumption that identification and role modelling are what make mentoring work.

The research went on next to evaluate the effects of the sex of the mentor and the type of mentoring function performed. Protégés were asked to give their response to the statement 'My career is moving along much faster than that of other women of my age and experience'. The results clearly showed that it was not the sex of the mentor but the functions provided by the mentor that account for whether one sees one's career in the fast lane or not. Mentor functions accounted for almost 20 per cent of the variance in perception of career progress.

In order to determine whether sexuality created insuperable barriers to male-mentored females, the researchers asked both mentors and protégés: 'Does this relationship have any significant impact on other relationships in your life?' Jealous spouses were mentioned by three of the mentors and two of the protégés. One of the mentors stated, 'At first my wife was jealous because the name of my protégé kept cropping up in conversation. I have now stopped talking about her at home'. Another stated: 'Yes, at times I've had problems with my wife. I think it's hard for women to accept this kind of relationship but I think I've resolved it'.

A second problem, that of snide remarks from co-workers, fell more heavily on the shoulders of the protégés than those of the mentors. Comments from the protégés included: 'I've heard rumbles about how we had this intense affair, it just isn't true'. People say 'How is the romance?'; 'In the beginning there were a lot of comments like 'Did you sleep with him to get the job' – I don't hear them much any more'.

The causes of family resentment surrounding mentor demands on protégés time and energy were not always clear. One protégé said, 'I worried about how my husband might take it. My mentor demands total devotion to the job'. Another confided her fears, 'I worried that sex might enter into the relationship but neither of us ever allowed that to happen'. Yet a third stated: 'I work very hard and long hours. Sometimes my husband thinks my job is more important to me than the family. Some days it is'. These comments only arose from pairs where the mentor was male.

One additional, and major, problem experienced by protégés was another kind of jealousy. That was the envy exhibited by the co-workers of one third of the respondents. The protégé was perceived as receiving preferential treatment from the boss. This emotion affected those mentored by female and male equally. Several of the respondents felt that the mentoring relationship had also been of benefit to other relationships both at work and outside. When male-mentored women identified a positive result at work they all indicated that the mentoring increased their acceptance or stature amongst colleagues. One protégé noted

Other attorneys in the firm accept me better; my mentor is considered a leader and for him to be my advocate has been positive. Other supervisors come to me for help in presenting their cases to him and it has also helped me to deal more effectively with the men in the company for which I work.

Three protégés mentioned assorted non-work benefits; 'A close relationship has developed between our families' and 'I don't know whether it is the relationship or the fact that I have been doing different things. I have much broader horizons now'. Those mentored by females mentioned a more diverse set of work and non-work benefits. About work they noted: 'It has helped me function more effectively at work, even during a bad personal time.' and 'It made it possible for me to mentor a young man.' About other aspects of their lives they said, 'I now move in an entirely different circle. I have even changed who I want to be. An enormous impact! She makes sure I meet people'; and 'It gave me courage to go through my divorce and to get on with my life'; 'At home she is my role model' and 'The relationship has made me more confident with people on the outside'.

Mentors also noted some interesting effects on other relationships in their lives. One male mentor states: 'It has been positive at home, my wife has great respect for my protégé. It also reinforces my image with my peers that I encourage women to do things' and 'Without my protégé, and her way of dealing with people, there would be a tremendous vacuum in my life. She has a capacity for affirming me in a way that has helped me to live a more balanced life'.

The reactions of two female mentors illustrate both work and non-work dividends: 'It has relieved a lot of stress for me to have my protégé on board. Cliques are forming, those that we can work with and those we can't' and 'at home there have been good feelings, my daughter is very close to her'.

From their collected data, the researchers summarised the problems and benefits of mentoring.

Problems

There are sex-related problems unique to cross-sex mentoring, and they affect relationships both at work and at home. They feel, however, that the problem may be exaggerated as most of the participants in the study had succeeded in dealing with those problems. Even the most frequently mentioned problem (by observers) that of the jealous spouse, emerged in only a small fraction of the male/female relationships.

The greatest single problem, again arising in only a fraction of the relationships, is the resentment of co-workers. Both male/female and female/female relationships had to cope with this.

Benefits

Both mentors and protégés often mentioned benefits to their work or non-work relationships which appeared to largely offset any problems that may be experienced.

When the researchers presented their findings to managers they found that the managers took one of two extreme positions on mentoring. They were either totally positive or totally negative. Those on the positive side often went to the point of advocating that every new manager who joined the organisation should be assigned to a mentor. Although mentoring may be valuable to some, not everyone has the personality to be either a good mentor or protégé. It is felt that mutual identification may be a necessary first phase of the relationship, and taking into account the sensitive issues which can develop in cross-gender mentoring, it may seem presumptuous for managers to dictate who mentors whom.

Conversely, given the obvious value of mentoring in developing young people, it would seem to be counter-productive for managers to exclude mentoring entirely from their management development programmes. The researchers finally recommend the following points for consideration.

1. Recognise the relevance of mentoring and encourage it amongst those who can benefit from such a relationship. Do this in such a way that those who do not choose to enter this kind of relationship are not penalised, in terms of organisational rewards or access to other developmental opportunities.
2. Provide counselling and training to current and potential mentors in order to develop their skills in the mentoring role.
3. Provide opportunities for potential protégés to interact with and show their potential to senior personnel who are prospective mentors. An example of such a mechanism is the well-known McCormick 'multiple management' scheme where committees of junior managers study organisational problems and recommend solutions to the levels of management responsible.
4. Lead the way in legitimising mentoring within the organisation. Mentoring relationships become a problem when the participants feel they must keep their relationship 'in a closet'. Secrecy, conspiracy, gossip, suspicion and an immense amount of wasted energy are the inevitable results if mentoring relationships are not seen as acceptable in terms of management values and the norms of the organisational culture.

A good example of a successful mentoring programme is that installed and designed by Merrill Lynch in New York as part of their Management Readiness Programme. This is a six-month career development programme to which a formal mentoring programme was added:

1. to help generate high-level management support and visibility,
2. to build bridges between high-level managers and employees,
3. to help participants learn about the firm's culture,
4. to provide opportunities for talented people developers to be seen.

The mentors are departmental or higher level managers who volunteered to act as counsellors and advisers to four people during the six month programme. The members of each 'quartet' all came from different areas of the company, but never from the same area as the mentor. Mentors agree to meet with their quartets about once a month, either in group or individual meetings.

Before the start of each programme mentors are given general guidelines to follow and a former mentor comes in to discuss activities and to answer questions. Mentors are urged to use their individual strengths and to encourage the group members to take as much initiative as possible. They are also encouraged to talk to the participants' managers at least once so that the managers do not feel left out.

Each mentor has different strengths and each quartet has different needs and no two groups have had the same experience. The most common activities to date have included the following:

1. Advice about career paths and how to move ahead at Merrill Lynch.
2. Assistance with developmental planning.
3. Tours of such areas of interest as the New York Stock Exchange, regional operational centres, computer services and sales offices.
4. Discussion of such topics of interest as planning, budgeting, networking and the structure of the company.

Some of the more interesting experiences are as follows:

Some mentors encourage each member of the quartet to take full responsibility for running a meeting. When one group wanted to learn about regional operational centres, one participant planned an agenda, engaged a speaker and provided a slide presentation. She then wrote up the experience and shared it with all participants and mentors through the programme newsletter.

Many mentors and protégés have established special, ongoing relationships. One black woman, who had never before developed a comfortable relationship with a senior-level manager, was able to establish a highly rewarding relationship with her white male mentor. After one frank discussion on black–white relationships, she felt so good that she bought him a copy of *Black Life in Corporate America* as a gift.

Some mentors set up introductions for individuals who want to explore new areas of the firm. One mentor asked each protégé to give him three areas of interest and then set up appointments with individuals he knew would be helpful. Mentors reported that they gained a lot from the experience, although some wished that they had been able to devote more time to their quartet. Some typical comments were:

'It made me realise some of my own deficiencies and I am now working on those areas.'

'I saw the need to develop my own people more clearly than ever.'
'It is an ego-booster.'
'I got more feedback on certain topics from these individuals that I do from my own staff.'
'I feel a sense of pride in helping Merrill develop future managers.'

In evaluating the programme the protégés say that they too have gained a great deal from the programme. Many go so far as to say that the mentor relationship has been one of the most beneficial parts of the entire six-month programme. Some of their comments are listed below:

'I now have a much better understanding of how the firm works. My mentor gave me a behind-the-scenes glimpse of how various people have succeeded and how the various areas interrelated.'
'I liked having someone in upper management to talk frankly to about job problems. I am now acting as a mentor for non-exempt employees in my department.'
'The mentor gave me a more realistic view of my career goals and helped me build confidence in myself as an individual and as a manager.'

It is felt that mentoring programmes have more chance of succeeding if the mentors are voluntary participants. Mentoring in a formal programme takes time and commitment to human resource development. At Merrill Lynch the career development co-ordinator talks to all mentor applicants before making the final selection. She describes the time involved, as well as past problems and challenges and at the same time answers questions. She also tries to uncover any 'arm twisting' or ambivalence about the six-month commitment.

Merrill Lynch also aim to minimise the rules and maximise the mentor's personal freedom. They feel that there is a fine line between too much structure and not enough. At the beginning of the programme mentors were given a two-inch binder with suggested activities, exercises, instruments and readings as well as a briefing on ways to use them. Now, two years after the beginning of the programme, they still have a briefing and receive the binder, but are urged to find out what works for them and to build on their own management style. Past mentors answer questions and problem solve with new mentors.

Mentors are encouraged to create networking opportunities for protégés across functional areas and hierarchical layers. They feel that this is particularly important for equal opportunity requirements. Breaking into the informal decision-making process is very important for career mobility.

Merrill Lynch also feel that a potential pitfall of a formal mentoring programme is that protégés may want and expect more than mentors can deliver and they recommend that participants should keep their expectations at a modest level. The amount of time and energy a mentor can deliver is limited. Protégés are encouraged to clarify exactly what they want from the mentor in their first communication session. Once these views have been exchanged the sessions can be scheduled to meet everyone's needs.

The company also rewards its mentors and works to increase their visibility not only by publicly linking their success to the success of the programme but in other, more tangible ways:

1. Mentors' names are on the written summaries of individual accomplishments that are circulated throughout the company at the conclusion of each programme.
2. Mentors attend the graduation banquet and receive a token gift and a personal thank-you from senior level executives.
3. Mentors' ideas, accomplishments and activities are recorded in a bimonthly newsletter.

The direct managers of the programme participants sometimes feel left out. They have never had a six-month development programme and they have never been given a high-level mentor. To help ease these problems, the mentor is encouraged to telephone each protégé's manager and become acquainted. The mentor, managers and MRP participants meet informally during the six-month period and both mentor and protégé keep the manager informed of what they are doing. Protégés also get specific input from the manager on their development plan and final profile statement. This three-way dialogue increases the chance that the development plan will really work and address the correct area. Manager/mentor involvement also builds communication links and turns the manager into an ally instead of a potential adversary.

The mentoring approach, as with any idea, must be allocated a reasonable amount of time if it is to succeed. It will need to be carefully evaluated and periodically up-dated in order to meet the changing needs of the organisation. Both mentors and protégés will need to find an appropriate balance between intimacy and distance that facilitates learning, growth and productivity. There are considerable benefits, however, for the companies who operate such schemes. Mentoring fosters the development of human resources by linking high-potential employees, both female and male, with proven, skilled high-level managers. In this way the company culture is passed on, loyalty to the company is developed and the accepted organisational norms are inculcated. Above all mentoring is a cost-effective way to keep the top people motivated by exposing them to individuals who will look up to them and expose them to the ideas of a younger generation.

10 Networking: 'A Tool for Transformation'

The subject of networking has become rather overworked during the 1980s. It was at one time confined to the view of 'the old boy network' stemming from public school contacts and the gentleman's club. Today the term pervades all areas of communication from TV networks to computer networking as well as referring to bodies of people who belong to a network formed for a specific purpose.

One of the most significant developments in the process of networking over recent years has been the growth of mutual-help networks. These have been described as: 'Our healthy response to the remoteness of modern institutions, a move towards greater power and resources for the individual.' Marilyn Ferguson in her celebrated book *The Aquarian Conspiracy* says 'The network is the antidote to alienation. It generates enough power to remake society. It offers the individual emotional, intellectual, spiritual and economic support . . . it is the institution of our time, an open system, a dissipative structure . . . poised for reordering, capable of endless transformation.' Where the original old-boy network reinforced exclusivity and self-protection, the new networks are formed to extend opportunity by opening out communication systems. Through networking individuals gain access to the information and contacts which can enhance their ability to share ideas and to take positive action.

Why women need networks

Over the past few years there has been a substantial growth in the number of networks formed to help women with their careers. These range from in-house networks like Women in BP or the Boots Women Returners' Network to professional networks like Women in Banking or Women in Media. There are also business and training networks like

NOWME (National Organisation for Women's Management Education) or Women and Training which are designed to promote wider links for women across industries and encourage specialist training for women.

All these networks have a common aim: to further the opportunities for women in their careers by providing support and contacts. They have become established to combat the sense of isolation many women feel either as a working minority within an industry or in wanting to break out of the traditional mould of assistant and supporter rather than leader. They are neither radical feminist movements nor ladies clubs but seek only to help women recognise their potential to create a more fulfilled working life.

Some of these networks are quite conservative in their operation believing that it is the individual's responsibility to further their development. They are less likely to see problems of advancement in terms of the general structure of business but rather as the need for women to cultivate their own skills and experience. These networks act as a forum for women to share ideas and exchange news rather than as the focus for a cause. The more radical networks carry an element of compaigning for a better deal for women like the 300 Group which is designed to encourage more women to enter the field of politics and takes its name from an overall aim to see a 50 per cent ratio of women representing the nation in the Houses of Parliament. One of the oldest networks in this category is the Fawcett Society which was founded in 1866 to fight sex discrimination and is still doing battle.

One of the main functions of women's networks is to foster a sense of co-operation. Women have always been prepared to help each other out in the home. Social networks are spontaneously formed around the baby clinics and the school gates which give rise to practical support like baby-sitting circles, car rotas or child sharing. These networks have become an invaluable substitute for the extended family, combating the extreme isolation felt by many young mothers. They reach their peak during the early school days by which time strong and binding links have often been formed between mothers who may well remain friends for life. However, as the children get older and women begin to look for work these networks slowly fade as their members become scattered. Some move house, some take part-time work, others begin studying or return to full-time work. There becomes very little time for socialising because the demands of combining the two activities take over. For those women who go back to work there is the recurrence of the sense of isolation in an environment from which they have been absent for several years.

Networks can be seen as an important source of support for several categories of women.

The woman returner

Of all the phases of women's career development this is probably the most difficult one. As we saw from the chapter on Women Returners, even a comparatively short period away from work can have a devastating effect on women's confidence causing them to lower their expectations of what they can achieve. This effect is compounded by the inflexibility of working patterns generally where continuous full-time employment is viewed as the norm. Women at this point are faced with two structural barriers: how to get back on to the rungs of a career structure and how to combine work with caring for a family. For many women the choice of career may have changed as a result of the break from work. This presents a further problem of deciding what else to do. Whereas a young woman may have been happy to work as a reception-ist, secretary or shop assistant, with maturity she can feel she would like a more challenging career, especially if this is likely to span a further 25 years. She is then faced with making a choice about retraining or extending her education to improve her chances for a better job.

Women at this stage generally feel totally separated from the world of work and out of touch with the latest developments. They often feel that things have changed even more than the reality because their confid-ence has been considerably reduced. Simply knowing where and how to start looking for work can become a major hurdle unless help and support is available. Networks for these women are an invaluable resource for making the transition back to work. Access to information and contacts provide the bridge they need to cross the river of uncertainty.

Many of the established networks are open to women returners. The professional networks are specially helpful to women who know what they want to do but need to update skills and knowledge. They offer the chance to find out what developments there have been in the field and what jobs may be available. The business and training networks are often geared to giving special help to women returners with talks and courses to help establish confidence and business skills. Women in Management have a high proportion of women returners who are members as does Women and Training.

Women returners network

This special network was established specifically to help women wanting to return to work. Founded in 1984 by a group of educationists, they take a special interest in government issues relating to women's access to education, training and work. At the same time it offers a networking resource for its members providing information and contacts. In particular they believe that lack of information hinders women's progress and would like to see a national service established to help adults identify relevant courses for employment training. In their first year they were sponsored by the EOC and employed two women returners to survey education and training opportunities for women returning to work in England and Wales. The results were published by Longmans as a directory: *Returning to Work: Education and Training for Women* which has a very comprehensive list of courses available for women in all parts of the UK.

Career developers

As we have seen from the figures a high proportion of women are employed at the lower end of the career structure. Many see very little opportunity of making progress believing that their services and contributions go unrecognised. Networking for these women can bring about a real change in outlook by making them aware of their own responsibility for change. A greater sense of power and the possibility of change is brought about by groups of women being able to meet and discuss the issues faced at work. Within company networks women have the opportunity to meet and talk with more senior members of staff. These more experienced members have usually joined the network because they are committed to helping others and will therefore offer advice on how to improve promotion prospects within the company. The shared gossip on staff movements and company policy developments leads to a greater awareness of where opportunities lie and how to take advantage of them. Speakers from other organisations can add new perspectives on career development. Ideas for company training for women can be put forward and suggested to management. In this way internal networks can provide a united voice for female employees and their special interests.

Career changers

Like the career developers, women in this category are usually looking for ways of improving their prospects. They will usually look to external networks for ideas and contacts in the areas into which they are considering a move. By meeting other women in a cross-section of industries they are able to gain a sense of what will be involved in a new career. They will discover what routes to pursue and what qualifications may be necessary.

Women in Management have a special subgroup for women in this position which meets in members' houses. This provides an enormous source of encouragement for women to put action into their plans.

A recent article in the Women in Management newsletter demonstrated the value of the membership directory given to all members. One member, seeking to change her career, used her directory to make contact with other members who worked in the business she had chosen to move into, computers, and set about contacting them for advice. The result was a lunch date with a member whose help led to the finding of a new job. Although the writer demonstrated that she had taken most of the initiative in seeking to make a change she had been helped enormously by being able to use contacts.

Women alone

For some women reaching the top can be a very lonely process, especially where she is surrounded by male colleagues. These women have a special need to meet with and exchange views with other women in similar positions. Professional networks offer this kind of contact and they can become quite powerful organisations like the City Women's Network which holds monthly luncheons in the livery hall usually with a guest speaker. NOWME has a special role to play for women who work alone, especially as consultants or trainers for women managers. Working alone can be very isolating but by taking part in a professional network consultants have the opportunity of meeting businesswomen in senior positions often to mutual business advantage.

Network contacts are also very important to the increasing numbers of women who live alone. When problems arise at work it can be stressful not to be able to come home and vent one's feelings to a partner who is willing to listen. Network contacts can fill this gap where bonds have been formed and confidentiality is assured. The fact that women may be in similar working roles means there will be a greater degree of empathy shared and perhaps constructive advice offered.

Networking power

As you can see from the above examples, networks function at a variety of levels to help their members. They are not clubs because they are formed to further the interests of the individual members rather than a common cause. They are not there to raise funds and provide a good time for all (although these may be by-products); they are there to improve the career and business prospects of their members. They act as a linking agent to enable members with mutual interests to foster creative relationships. They are designed to encourage members to make and use contacts, to give as well as receive, to be active rather than passive. Each network has its own style of doing this but ultimately their aim is to spread power by sharing information and resources. Although some may carry a degree of exclusivity, if just because they are women only networks, most are committed to the ideal of power sharing. They see women's development as the means to share power more evenly which is why training in skills like negotiation, public speaking and assertiveness are offered by many of them.

The power of these networks has been enhanced by the public image many have created. Many are recognised by authorities like the Training Agency, the British Institute of Management and the Industrial Society as well as the media. Some have direct sponsorship from major companies who recognise their achievements and support their aims. In fact many of the networks are run by women who have a high status within industry. Jane Kelly, chairman of Women in Management, is in fact a director of AMI Health Care plc and she puts her chairman's responsibilities high on her list of priorities. She is committed to the view that successful women have an important role in helping other women to develop as mentors, role models, advisers or simply networkers.

The European Women's Management Development Network

The influence of women's networks is spread far beyond the boundaries of one country and transnational networking has become an important mechanism for building cultural bridges by identifying common problems and issues for women in business. EWMD was created in 1984 under the auspices of the European Foundation for Management Development (EFMD). Its declared objective is: 'To contribute to the improvement of the quality of management in Europe by developing and promoting the full potential of women managers'. The organisation feels strongly that this will be achieved in the following ways.

1. By identifying and promoting best practices for women's manage-

ment development, at the same time contributing to knowledge about management practices and theories in general.

2. By publicising women's achievements in management and encouraging women to seek opportunities.

3. By supporting and co-operating with national and other networks with similar objectives.

4. By providing forums for collecting and exchanging information about women's management development in Europe and internationally.

Members are offered four main services:

1. A directory of members including information on professional qualifications, activities, interests, languages spoken and relevant prior experience.

2. A regular newsletter containing reports of individual member countries, guest articles, training news, book abstracts and reviews and details of past and planned events.

3. The Annual Conference of the association provides an excellent opportunity for all members to meet on a regular basis. Organised each year in a different country in Europe, it takes as its theme a topic of current interest to women's management development with appropriate members and invited guests as speakers and workshop leaders. The conference is of a uniformly high standard, simultaneous multi-lingual translation is available for both plenary and workshop sessions and delegates are normally warmly welcomed and entertained by the host country. The conference papers are published as a report.

4. The General Assembly of the Association, held during the Annual Conference, offers every member the opportunity to share their ideas on activities of the network and to make suggestions for the future.

Members also organise local events. Visits from overseas members are also used as an opportunity to bring an interest group together. Membership is open to both organisations and any person having a professional interest in the field. The two categories of membership are:

1. *Individual members*. Any person having a professional interest in the activities of the association can become a member. The existing

membership includes managers, consultants, trainers, educationists and researchers.

2. *Institutional members.* Corporations, educational bodies, government or international bodies and voluntary organisations concerned with women's management development can become institutional members of the association.

Membership of this kind of network provides a ideal opportunity to forge real and lasting links with like-minded people within the European Community. The directory provides a ready-made list of contacts for anyone moving to another part of Europe, either on regular short business trips or for longer work assignments. The conferences provide an opportunity to compare management development in other European countries with our own and as such is helping to bridge the divide between the different member countries of the EEC. A complete list of UK, European and US representatives will be found at the end of the book.

Making a network function effectively

There is a fine line between running a network successfully and making networking successful. It is quite possible to run a network which serves as a meeting point for women, make it more interesting by adding a speaker and sociable by offering drinks and snacks. Members may be quite satisfied that they have had a pleasant evening's entertainment without feeling moved to do anything further until the next meeting. By these standards nothing much has changed for those who have attended, very little, if any, action will take place as a result of the meeting.

We have used Marilyn French's phrase 'A tool for transformation' to open this chapter because it underlines the significance of networking. A network must be a change agent if it is not to be a club, a society or an association. It must be dynamic as a motivational force which encourages women to be more active in the process of self-development. It must promote the activity of making contact with other members and strengthening the links between women. It should demonstrate how information exchange can create opportunities and openings for which women can actively prepare themselves by training and education. It should use the common experiences of women as a basis for discussion and ideas for change. It should provide a platform for ideas to be distilled and converted into action.

Network aims and objectives

Good networking practice begins with the formation of objectives for the organisation. In most cases the written aims of women's networks contain axis words for women's development. For example, the European Foundation For Women's Management Development (EFWMD) aims are to: 'Contribute to the improvement of the quality of management by developing and promoting the full potential of women as managers.' NOWME aims: 'to inform and encourage the growing number of women seeking to make a career in management. It also serves as a resource to organisations, personnel managers and individuals who are keen to develop their staff. Additionally NOWME is a national network for members.'

Women in Management was originally founded to bring pressure to bear on employers to make more effective use of their women managers. It was founded by Eleanor McDonald and has now been in operation for twenty years and has a current membership of 800. The experience and maturity of the organisation provides a model for good networking practice. In 1986 the aims of the organisation were revised:

1. To become a major influence in public affairs on all matters relevant to women in management.
2. To train and develop women through their various activities and with corporate sponsorship.
3. To provide and disseminate information in the widest sense and to use the association as a central reference point.
4. To create opportunities for networking via their evening and luncheon meetings and other special events.
5. To act as mentors so that women obtain the help and assistance they need from within the supportive group of WIM.

These examples reflect the general principles of women's networks' promotion of women's career development. They demonstrate the dynamic nature of networking as a means of motivating and informing women of ways to develop. They are instrumental in the process of continuous development which is increasingly being recognised by employers as an important part of staff training. It is for these reasons that more companies are willing to support external networks and develop their own in-house networks.

Network formation

Networks are essentially self-generating, formed by and run through their members, usually on a voluntary basis. In most cases they begin with the ideas of a group of innovative women who meet to discuss current issues concerning women in employment. This group forms the impetus for network organisation, first discussing common networking aims and then preparing plans for extending their activities. NOWME, for example, began life with a weekend conference at a management centre with 30 participants, mainly women involved in management training. They had come together to discuss the needs and problems of women managers in the 1980s but agreed that a talking shop was insufficient. A fifteen-point agenda for action was proposed which included the organisation of NOWME. It took two years to establish NOWME as a properly constituted company but the 60 founder members guaranteed its financial existence. From this early solid commitment the organisation has been able to grow and develop, expanding both its membership and activities. Like many of the current women's networks, NOWME was formed in 1980 at a time when five years of the Sex Discrimination Act had been in operation with very little impact on opening up women's opportunities. Where legislation has failed to produce change the networks have been a major force of inspiration to women themselves to initiate the necessary changes. The founder members determine the style of the network and become role models for other women who participate. The strength of the network will come from the strengths of its members who must generate the active involvement of new members. The leaders must create the vision for others to follow and encourage fresh blood and new ideas to ensure its continued success.

Financing the networks

Most of the external networks are financed largely by their membership fees and additional charges made for group meetings. Costs are kept low because organising members usually give their services voluntarily. The fees may vary considerably according to the status, willingness and ability of members to pay. Some organisations charge a high member ship fee to preserve a degree of exclusivity like Network, founded in 1981 for high-powered businesswomen to ensure 'women's contribution and influence is recognised as a vital force in all the corridors of power'. Other networks are able to keep their costs low by appealing for corporate sponsorship. WIM is supported by at least 15 major companies, including BP, National Westminster, RTZ and American Express. Women and Training have funding from the Training Agency although sadly this is to be gradually reduced as part of the Government's strategy to make organisations self-supporting. The Women Returners Network was helped in its first year by sponsorship from the EOC. More sponsorship from industry should be encouraged wherever possible if women's networks are to reach beyond the privilege of those already employed in successful careers. Only with financial backing can they extend their services in training and spread information to women with potential. Women returners can rarely afford the high cost of management training from their own resources and yet this is often the very tool they need in order to make progress. For many companies the cost of sponsorship is minimal compared with the benefits which may be accrued by increasing the pool of skilled labour. As we have already acknowledged, women are needed by industry in greater numbers than ever since the Second World War. Networks have become established for women's management development but there are signs this movement may extend to other skills areas to encourage women of all capacities to improve their skills and return to work.

As far as internal networks are concerned this is probably one of the most effective ways of encouraging employee development and training. Women within a company are usually prepared to give their own time to attend meetings and help run the network. The cost to the company is in providing the resources necessary for holding meetings and communicating the activities. Tesco, for example, have their own training centre which is used for evening meetings.

Network information

One of the most crucial aspects to running a successful network is the ability to spread information. It is lack of information that inhibits the power of many women to progress. Knowing what is available and knowing what can be achieved are the first steps to being motivated to take action. An effective network must not only act as an information resource but it must also have the ability to regularly transmit that information to its members. There are three main ways in which networks do this.

1. *Newsletters*
Most networks send out a regular newsletter to all their members on a regular basis. These contain details of meetings, courses, events and

books of interest to members. They also feature articles on current research into women's training and company initiatives for equal opportunities. Another popular feature is the case histories of successful women who serve as a role model for aspiring women managers. One of the most successful newsletters in this field has been 'Women & Training News' which is very widely circulated because it has been sponsored by the Training Agency and, over a period of over ten years built up a circulation figure of 12,000. This has served as an invaluable resource for all women concerned with career development either on a personal level or as trainers and consultants. One of its main functions has been to network the networks by giving regular details on the background and activities of other women's networks.

The most effective newsletters are those that draw on members experiences for copy. Members should be encouraged to take up their pens and express their views or tell their stories as a source of encouragement for other members. In this way the spirit of true networking, of active participation, is encouraged. There is always the danger of editorial exclusivity in compiling a newsletter where expediency takes precedence over general involvement. If ordinary members can see their views published they will be motivated to write rather than see the same names regularly printed. This process is encouraged by regular appeals to members to submit copy with suggestions and ideas on issues that would be relevant.

2. *Members directory*
Networking can only take place if access to members names, addresses and telephone numbers is readily available. This can best be achieved by publishing a directory containing all this essential information. Amendments can be distributed when subscriptions have been renewed. This, of course, is a time consuming and costly process but it is too important to be overlooked. Ideally, details of each member's company and position should be included with any special interests they may have noted. This will enable members to seek out sources of help or advice whenever necessary.

Keeping up to date with members details is a regular job but must necessarily take place for the mailing and subscription lists. With word processing facilities at the disposal of so many offices and individuals today it should not prove too difficult to provide this service to members.

3. *Meetings*
Regular meetings are essential to networking as a means of stimulating interpersonal contact. Although speakers are a popular attraction there

must also be time for members to mix. One of the best ways to achieve this is to appoint an experienced network member as a doorkeeper to meet members as they arrive to make sure they are introduced to someone else. This is not only welcoming but it also helps to break the ice as someone new enters the room. Ideally there is time at the beginning and the end of a talk for socialising informally, perhaps over refreshments.

There are other more formal methods to promote exchange of contacts. One is to use the topic in hand as a starting point for discussion before asking members to form small groups in which to raise further issues and then give feedback to the floor. This has proved to be a very successful method of ensuring that members learn something about each other and regularly results in an exchange of business cards or telephone numbers. Many network members will agree that this can be the most stimulating part of the evening enabling them to leave with the feeling that they have achieved something by making contacts.

The timing of meetings varies between networks; some take place over lunch although the majority are during the early evening when members can attend straight after work. It is important to gain some consensus of the most convenient time for meetings. If necessary these times can be alternated so as not to preclude a group of women who find one time inconvenient. Sometimes workshops or courses are better held over the weekend when children may be cared for by fathers or work is not interrupted. Like all working organisations networks are only as good as the people who participate in them. It is therefore imperative that each person who joins understands from the very start their personal role in building its success. Without this general commitment the organisers will be left with a mammoth task of servicing members without adequate support. In too many cases networks are treated by new members as clubs in that they pay their subscription and wait for things to be sent to them. The skill of the organisers is in harnessing the experience and talents of members for the common good. This can be achieved by:

1. Noting on membership applications what experience new members may have to offer.
2. Delegating roles to as many members as possible, however small, to ensure they take some part in the activities.
3. Utilising members' skills, experience and contacts in the creation of workshops, seminars or conferences.

4. Auditing the needs of members by questionnaires, or asking for input at meetings.

5. Encouraging written contributions to the newsletter on their experiences of say combining family and work, returning to work or changing direction.

6. Demonstrating in the newsletter or at meetings the positive benefits achieved by network members through network participation, e.g. where one member has been able to help another.

7. Offering incentives for members to recruit new members.

8. Encouraging members to seek sponsorship through their companies or any other organisations where they may have contacts.

9. Making appeals on behalf of members who need specific help.

10. Asking members to do research on issues which affect women, e.g. local colleges or courses.

11. Asking specific members to review books, publications or events.

The future of networking

Women's networks have grown in both strength and numbers over the last few years and the trend looks set to continue. They are popular because they fill an obvious gap in the help offered to women who face special difficulties with regard to work. By creating cheap and ready access to information and genuine contacts who are willing to help and advise others they provide an invaluable service. Active participation in a network is a learning experience in itself, one in which women are able to create and maintain plans for personal development while learning more about their needs and their potential. The major change necessary for the future is to give women more power so that they can play a more influential role in the business of the future – networks have become one of the most effective ways to achieve this.

Women in BP, now with eight years of experience in hand, report some of the ways in which their network has achieved this. Their strategy has been to help all women at all levels to develop their potential within BP. Their meetings have been used as a focus for training and development themes explaining what opportunities are open to women within the company. Practical help has been offered through speakers, debates and workshops on assertiveness and combining career and family. Study groups have been set up to investigate key issues which have resulted in practical action like the completion of an advice pack for women taking maternity leave or a 'self-development' advice pack. One group became involved in lobbying the Government on Personal Tax Reform for married women while another examined the issues of secretarial career development.

The influence of these groups and their reports has spread beyond the network boundaries to other employees, men as well as women, and has set a pattern for further studies on issues relating to all employees. A network directory has been set up to help members make contact with other individuals in the organisation and to strengthen the links with outside networks, schools and other educational organisations. A newsletter enables members to keep in touch with the various branches of the organisation from their research centre in Sunbury to as far afield as outposts in China and Holland. Above all, individual women feel able to find support, advice and ideas on how to establish and further their development aims. This is the power they need to transform their job into a career.

11 Corporate Husband – Corporate Wife

Although the career break taken for family reasons has shrunk from 14 years to less than five over the past two decades there is still a tendency for women to cling tenaciously to their old roles. The role of a career woman has been added to those of wife and mother and, perhaps as penance for apparently 'having it all', the majority of women are still attempting to 'do it all'. We were recently disturbed to find, on one of our courses, a young woman of 29 who had only recently recovered from a brain haemorrhage. When we questioned her about her lifestyle she admitted that she was responsible for taking her small son to his child-minder, before she went to her office each day. Her husband did not drive, was not interested in gardening and did not help with the housework. When we suggested that she should perhaps try to find some time just for herself she responded by planning to extend her daily two hours of housework to two and a half in order to buy some spare time at the weekend! It simply did not occur to the young lady in question that there were certain domestic chores which might be tackled by her partner although she had a very powerful argument in her favour, namely her own survival.

When the captains of industry are interviewed by the media they frequently pay homage to the support and encouragement which they have received from their wives over the years. 'I could never have achieved my success without her' is a frequent cry. When the few women to achieve director status face similar interviews they frequently admit that their husband is no longer *in situ* or alternatively they have never married at all, the hard work put into building the career simply left no time for the development of close personal relationships.

These stories are often repeated by women attending our courses and the adjective 'superwomen' is often appended to women who are attempting to combine a career and family life. The managing of the dual career family and the achievement of balance between work and home commitments, presenting as they do conflicting loyalties and priorities, is a necessary focus for the future if genuine equality of opportunity is to be achieved.

The Board of Esso UK, plc recognised this dilemma and now every member of the organisation has spent half a day discussing what equal opportunities means to them and coming up with practical plans for their own department. The work/family issues, career breaks, relocation and training are topics that come up again and again. Company-based crèches, child-minding allowances and all kinds of flexible working, however, are meaningless if the woman continues to shoulder the major burden for child and home care simply because 'it has always been this way'. If equal opportunities are to work in the future the renegotiation of domestic roles must begin now. Some men are already experimenting with role reversal and are opting to stay at home and take on the role previously undertaken by women.

This role reversal has sometimes begun as a temporary arrangement, following redundancy. In some cases the man has decided that he has had enough of the rat race or does not wish to continue to do a job that he no longer finds stimulating. Men frequently regard the care of children as relaxation or play and come to enjoy the new role so much that they opt for a permanent situation as house husband.

Lesley Garner, writing in *How to Survive As A Working Mother* says:

> Something in every working mother's life has to give. It is the working mother's number one task to make sure that it isn't her. What you allow to slide to the floor in your own overcrowded life is a matter of little choice guided by a lot of desperation. It may be cooking gourmet dinners or ironing your husband's shirts or reading the newspapers, but go it must. Priorities may be the key to avoiding guilt. They are also the key to surviving through the week.

Delegation and a fair distribution of labour appear to be the key elements in successful home management. Husbands should be encouraged in the belief that they are doing their share rather than 'lending a hand'. Children should be encouraged to take their share of the chores, even if their rooms become an occupational health hazard as a result.

If women insist on filling up the freezer before they leave on a business trip, or helping their partner to pack for his, the process of change will never begin. The daily 'to do' list for household chores should apply to all the members of the household and not just the working wife. The alternative to delegating to members of the family is to pay someone else to do the household chores. One of the growth areas in new businesses are support agencies for dual career families. There are companies who will take on the ironing, walk the dog, water the plants or take a child to hospital. There are others who will give your home a mega clean before your mother arrives for a holiday and individuals who enjoy gardening so much that they will happily care for yours. These services are not generally cheap but if they are paid for out of a joint income the financial burden become less onerous and the reduction in stress is an added bonus.

Child-care

In 1984 the Inland Revenue made a controversial decision that child-care facilities provided by employers should be taxed as a benefit in kind. Employees earning more than £8500 a year were to be taxed on this 'perk' in the same way that they would be taxed on the cost of private medical insurance. This decision was taken in spite of earlier assurances to the Equal Opportunities Commission that child-care was not a taxable benefit. As we write the Chancellor of the Exchequer is under pressure to reverse this decision. This tax is a disincentive to employers to provide work-place crèches and at the same time is hindering the return to work of many women with preschool children. It seems to be a short-sighted policy not to repeal this tax at a time when women's skills are needed more than ever before. (The staff restaurant and sports club are both subsidised benefits on which employees pay no tax.) A parliamentary question revealed that the cost of abandoning the tax on work-place nurseries would be no more than £1 million a year so the cost to the nation would not be prohibitive.

The tax issues do not end with work-place crèches. If a woman decides to pay for private child-care she pays from taxed income. She is providing employment and free meals; in some cases she is providing free accommodation (which means use of telephone, washing machine and sometimes a car). An experienced nanny from one of the three residential training colleges in the UK can command a salary of £150 per week. A newly qualified NNEB nanny will expect £65 per week in London and slightly less elsewhere. A daily nanny will expect between £20 and £30 per day for approximately a 10-hour working day. An au pair expects from £18–£25 per week but Home Office guidelines specify that she should only work 30 hours per week. Some working mothers are able to arrange to share a nanny with a friend or working colleague but this takes careful planning and organisation.

Compared with other member states of the EEC Britain lags behind when it comes to helping women to fulfil their potential at work and continue to raise the next generation. A recent report carried out for the European Commission points to the serious underfunding of child-care provision in the UK. Shared responsibilities for child-care in parental leave schemes, with time off work for either parent, are seen by EEC countries as a contributory factor towards strengthening family life and helping women to retain their career. Other major advantages are a reduction in unemployment, in some EEC countries, the parent on maternity or paternity leave is replaced by an unemployed worker. Skills and expertise in industry are retained, saving money on retraining and recruitment programmes.

In 1983 the European Commission published its proposals for a directive on parental leave. It offered a minimum of three months leave per worker, per child together with a sharing of child-care between fathers and mothers as a part-time option; plus a special leave allowance. This would help to end the precarious juggling of home and job. The job would not be jeopardised when parents had to put their family first and, most importantly, the major part of the responsibility for looking after a child need not fall on the mother's shoulders.

The aim was to establish a common statutory provision throughout the EEC, guiding the developing provisions of extended leave and ensuring that it was not discriminatory in any way. Most EEC countries now offer parental leave as a result. These provisions vary from ten weeks to three years. The UK and the Republic of Ireland were the only member states to veto the directive, twice in 1985 and again in 1986. They stated that parental leave would be too expensive, too unworkable and that it would damage job prospects by dissuading employers from taking on women. Because of this, only the forward-thinking employers in the UK offer parental leave or paternity leave. Penguin Books actually pioneered paternity leave at about the time of the EEC directive. Its paternity scheme was heralded as a 'model for negotiations in all areas of work'. The company offers ten days paternity leave for the first year of the child's life, additionally they offer 15 days compassionate leave granted at the discretion of management. Women can take one year off work with 25 weeks full pay and their old job remains open to them. The BBC offers five days paternity leave and gives sympathetic consideration to women who are unable to return to work full-time after childbirth by offering part-time work or a career break scheme.

Bronwen Cohen, head of the Policy Unit at the Equal Opportunities Commission, suggested at a recent conference at the Industrial Society that lack of parental provision goes a long way towards explaining why employment rates for mothers in Britain are among the lowest in the EEC. In 1986 the EOC carried out a survey which estimated that the likely cost to the government of introducing limited parental leave would be between £31 and £45 million. To offset this cost between 6000 and 9000 people a year could be removed from the dole queue as a result of jobs created by this scheme. Yet another EOC survey in 1983 found that 94 per cent of fathers took time off anyway, most between one and two weeks for child-care, with most of them losing annual leave or pay. Table 4 shows the position in the EEC as a whole.

Half the working mothers in the UK are not protected in their job unless they have the statutory two years qualifying service. The EOC in March 1988 recommended to the Home Secretary that the Employment Protection Act should be amended with no qualifying service to protect working mothers-to-be against unfair dismissal. Perhaps 1992 will be the time when the UK will bring its parental leave provision into line with the rest of Europe.

Company support for family problems

The American Express Company in the US discovered that help with family responsibilities was a major need for many of its employees. This discovery coincided with the evidence that the US labour market was shrinking and that by 1995, 85 per cent of new entrants would be women or ethnic minorities. This convinced the company that it had to take steps to ensure that it had a stable, productive workforce in the years ahead. Since that time American Express has implemented a range of initiatives including care centres for sick children and family seminars, to help employees cope with family responsibilities. However, we must stress that these initiatives are American and have not yet been implemented in Europe.

Jean Fraser, Corporate Vice-President, Employee Relations for Amex described the initiatives at the EFWMD Conference held in Brighton in 1987. It is important to realise that the US has no maternity leave provision which guarantees a job on returning to work. There are no funded day-care centres or crèches in the US in general, therefore it is more difficult to be a working mother in America than it is in the UK, although the general impression is that American women have it all. American Express has a female dominated workforce in the US, 57 per cent of their personnel are female compared with the average in other US companies which is 44 per cent. They are much more female than

Table 4 Parental leave in the EEC

Country	Maternity allowance/pay	Maternity grant	Parental leave
France	Offers 84 per cent of earnings for 16 weeks for insured women, includes adoptive mothers	£82 per month for one year from third months of pregnancy (mother must attend ante-natal class)	2 years unpaid parental leave or part-time work. Leave paid at £100 per month if 3 or more children
Italy	80 per cent of earnings for 5 months and 30 per cent of earnings for a further 6 months for employed women		Father or mother may take final 6 months at 30 per cent earnings
Denmark	90 per cent of average earnings for 28 weeks for employed and self-employed women, includes adoptive mothers		Up to 10 weeks of 28 can be taken by the father
Germany	100 per cent earnings for 14 weeks for insured women	£35 for insured women, £12–52 for low income families	10 months parental leave paid at £150 per month
Belgium	75 per cent of earnings for 14 weeks for insured women	First child £486, second child £335, subsequent children £180 for insured and low income families	6–12 months leave or the right to return to work part-time
United Kingdom	90 per cent of earnings for 6 weeks plus £32.85 for 12 weeks for insured women with 2 years service. £32.85 for 18 weeks for insured women with 6 months service. £30.05 for 18 weeks for recently insured women	£80 for low income families	

Source Personnel Today, 12 July 1988.

the average American Express company. They also have a large number of women in management with 40 per cent of management jobs being filled by women and a substantial number at senior level.

The Senior Vice-President, Jean's boss, is a woman who has earned the respect and trust of top level executives in the organisation. She also had her children while working at American Express and so is sympathetic to, and in tune with, the needs of working mothers. She also feels that it is critical that all the workforce should be helped and feels that productivity will suffer if they leave the organisation. As a first step to discovering what the needs of the workforce were, Jean did a survey of all the US employees on a voluntary basis. The finding told them a lot about the people who worked for them and Jean recommends this approach as a first step. They discovered that 32 per cent of their employees were married with children and 8 per cent were single parents (or 5000 people in a workforce totalling 55,000). Nineteen per cent had children under five and 9 per cent children under two, 38 per cent had a spouse or other relative at home caring for the children and 40 per cent of their employees paid for day-care of one kind or another. Only 6 per cent of employees have dependents other than a child or spouse, most of these are elderly parents and this percentage is expected to increase as the workforce ages. Four per cent are described as the 'sandwich generation' – they have both children and elderly relatives to care for and so are crunched up in the middle. We would like to point out that these statistics are based on 1986 data and these trends are now accelerating. As we write American Express are now doing a much more detailed survey on work and family issues to gain a better idea of employee critical needs. Some of the employee needs which American Express have already addressed, or are about to tackle, are listed below.

Resource and referral services
These help employees find child-care and elder-care services in their own communities.

Financial assistance
This includes benefit schemes, to help offset the cost of dependent care; subsidising the cost of day-care centres.

Time off and flexible time policies
These include family leave of absence with job guarantees; flexible work schedules; part-time work for professional/managerial staff; work-at-home arrangements.

Employee surveys
These assess the work/family needs of employees, so that appropriate policies and programmes can be developed.

Information seminars
These are lunchtime workshops for employees on a wide range of family related subjects.

Employee assistance programmes
These counsel and refer employees with personal or family problems.

Health and fitness programmes
These aim to improve the well-being of employees and alleviate stress.

On-site or near-site day-care centres
These are principally found in suburban or smaller urban locations; care centres for children are not company owned but the company sub-sidises employee access to them, for example in Florida American Express helped to fund the construction of a wing of a hospital and subsidises the fees that employees have to pay.

Sick-child services
These include special day-care centres; sections in hospitals; or in-home nursing care for mildly sick children.

'Latchkey' children
These consist of after-school programmes or services for children with no one at home until their parents return from work.

Relocation assistance for spouses
Provisions include preparation and help in finding jobs in the new location, school and other family-related information, as well as home-finding and home-selling schemes.

Philanthropic grants
These are funds to community-based organisations to increase and improve family services, such as day-care or care for the elderly.

Partnerships
These are coalitions between Government, other corporations and the community to address these issues.

The majority of British businesses are not initiating similar employee initiatives probably because there are fewer women in senior positions than in the US and women do not have the same power on a widespread basis as US women. British women are however collectively responsible for the current demographic changes which are just beginning to have an effect in the UK. This has at least begun to focus the minds of those involved in human resource planning and the British press is now beginning to write about family/work problems.

Managing the dual career

However well organised and happy the family unit is there will, almost inevitably, come a time when the question of relocation for career development reasons has to be considered. There has been a widespread belief that women lack mobility and this has been advanced as a reason for not promoting them to higher levels of management. Companies are also realising that men too have their reasons for not wishing to move. They have wives who work and children who may be at a critical stage in their education, making an unscheduled move generally undesirable. Some companies are already being forced to fill vacancies locally rather than move employees around the country.

In spite of this there are still 250,000 managers and professional workers who are now relocated each year. These relocations take place mainly within the UK although a few thousand are moved overseas, mainly to Canada and the US. Relocation is used to assist the development of high-flying managers, to ease skill shortages, to restructure business operations and to filter specialist knowledge through the organisation more swiftly.

The Institute of Manpower Studies has looked at reasons why professional people refuse relocation. The most frequent reason for refusing to move was that they were unwilling to move away from friends and relatives; the second most common reason was that their partner or children voted against the proposed move. Third on the list were environmental factors such as a less attractive new location or more expensive housing.

Those who take the plunge and agree to move do so for career development reasons, an increase in salary is the second consideration and good assistance with relocation expenses is the third. Most companies base their total relocation package on financial considerations. Research carried out by Merrill Lynch Relocation Management International into 305 British businesses found that 83 per cent of employers reimburse moving expenses, 34 per cent give mortgage assistance when employees move to a more expensive area and 60 per cent give some form of assistance with bridging loans.

Ginger Irvine is the founder and first president of FOCUS Information Services, a referral service for expatriates in London and is particularly sympathetic to the needs of the 'trailing spouse'. Focus carried out a survey of expatriates living in the UK. One of the questions asked was 'which area connected with the move was most frustrating for you?' The area which was of paramount importance was lack of communication from the employer or, where there was communication, it was not soon enough or thorough enough. She states quite categorically that the adaptation to the new environment has to begin before the move. The planning ahead is really important and the practical issues are urgent such as schooling, pets, where will I live, is there a hospital? The survey went on to ask 'who helped most before, during and after the move?' A number of choices were given and companies on the whole did not rate very highly. One woman rejected all the choices and simply wrote 'trial and error'. Companies tend to pay attention to the family during or just after relocation. By that time the financial investment in the individual is high and companies who frequently move their manager realise that it is during this time that pressures are most acute and they realise the necessity to guard against a change of mind on the part of the staff member involved.

Focus runs a telephone helpline, expatriates can ring up and ask for practical help such as where to find a plumber or a decorator, where to find a tax adviser or an orthodontist, where can we find children's drama classes and can you advise us on graduate programmes. You would not think that bringing a canary into the UK was high on the list of priorities but the question has been asked. Ginger stresses that distress in relocation comes from the frustration of time and energy lost in coping with the practical details of everyday life.

One company that gets a good star rating from at least one satisfied employee is IBM for when they relocated the husband they found a job for his wife. IBM has over 400,000 employees worldwide and almost 4000 of them are on relocated assignments at any one time. They have developed an international assignment plan and have established a worldwide network of people who are there to help. Relocation begins with 'preassignment activities', which are job planning discussions which take place with the manager. The employee is told what will be expected of her/him in the new job and from the new organisation. When this stage is completed a contract is signed and the employee goes on to meet four key contacts. The first is a Career Manager, this could be the existing manager or a level above. Other contacts are the International Assignment Representative (IAR), a work relocation manager and a work relocation international assignment representative in the work location country.

The IAR introduces the IBM international assignment plan contained in a large manual of information. A trip to the host country, lasting a week or longer, is arranged. In the host country the work location IAR is introduced and goes through his/her section of the international assignment plan. Merrill Lynch takes care of the housing problem and a visit to them is scheduled into the trip. A meeting is arranged with the work relocation manager and if necessary schools are seen. The overseas assignment is part of the career plan and this is discussed thoroughly with the career manager, these discussions include re-entry plans which involve thinking several years ahead. This is the preferred style of managing human resources for IBM and it speaks well for forward planning and the humane treatment of managers who face relocation. The international assignment plan contains much useful information including: pensions and insurances, who is taking care of the handling of belongings, what to do with the car, salary and service details, medical care, what to do with pets and information on schools. This comprehensive and sympathetic approach obviously goes a long way to help to alleviate the stress involved in relocation.

Dr Robin G. Lambert, a general practitioner writing to *The Times* on 28 October 1988 expressed the medical view of frequent relocation:

A great deal of mental and physical ill health in Britain is caused by frequent house moves. Much of the blame for this must be laid at the doors of our national firms, including insurance companies, banks and major businesses. In my work as a general practitioner I see families disrupted by repeated moves. The sequence starts with the husband's promotion from one area to another. Months may go by before his wife and children are able to move and live with him again. In the meantime he is, in effect, a single man, living away from home comforts. He is easy prey to an extra-marital affair, while his wife and family become used to life without him. When the family are reunited tensions develop because the individuals have established their own separate needs. Just as the husband/wife relationship is being re-established, the firm springs another move and the sequence starts all over again.

Extra-marital affairs and divorce run high in these groups and the resultant effects on all members of the family are seen in the GP's surgery. Even if the husband and wife remain loyal, the children are affected by frequent changes of school and friends, leading to poor performances, psychological problems and often delinquency. One accepts that promotion of personnel around the country is essential in these large organisations, but I have long felt that the frequency and number of these moves is unnecessary, and imposed on the employee with little or no thought for the well being of the individual and his family. Woe betide the employee who turns down such a move. This is a potent source of ill-health in Britain, and I feel that urgent consideration should be given at the highest levels of business to halt the perpetuation of this system. I have a blacklist of the worst offenders!

Most of us would agree with the content of Dr Lambert's letter but perhaps not quite so readily with the focus? However, Dr Lambert has admitted, via subsequent correspondence with us that career wives and trailing spouses can suffer similar problems.

Dr Annette Lawson has recently completed a six-year study of adultery and discovered that, in her study of 579 married women and men, 60 per cent of married men and 40 per cent of married women admitted to adulterous affairs. Other studies have shown that 50 per cent of married men and 40 per cent of married women commit adultery. To put it another way, in every other marriage someone at sometime is unfaithful.

The reasons that people begin their affairs vary, although 44 per cent of men and women in the study said that their sexual needs were not being met in marriage. Others, including some men but rather more women said that they desperately wanted companionship and appreciation; there were other women who, following the often expressed male view, felt entitled to seek sexual gratification with no strings outside the traditional marriage.

Lawson makes a very interesting comment that many marriages make women feel vulnerable, dependent and even powerless, but adultery has the opposite effect. Women feel that they have the power to begin or end a relationship.

Dr Lawson found that most affairs began opportunistically, because people found themselves in situations which offered temptation, and work is a prime example of this kind of opportunity. The projected increase of women into the labour market may provide more opportunity for women to become adulteresses.

Dr Lawson further found that the pain which can mar the pleasure of adultery seemed to deter few and almost no one said it was not worth it. It is the fact that adultery undermines society and risks everything, which makes it so exciting. It is dangerous passion and as such cannot be bought along with the Porsche and the smart flat in Chelsea Harbour.

Jeanette Taudin Chabot described in honest detail her version of a dual career family as Living Apart Together. Speaking at the EFWMD Conference in Brighton she expressed her surprise when one of her friends showed envy that Jeanette was able to build up her business tremendously during her husband's absence from home for a two-year overseas assignment. Jeanette felt that she had played superwoman with a superload, running the household on her own, coping with two teenage sons and dividing the rest of her time between business meetings and social commitments. In spite of the workload she felt a new freedom inside her marriage; 'I could keep on working through the night, clean the bathroom at midnight, invite people round for whatever reason, add to that the joy of reading in bed to my heart's content without worrying about someone turning over restlessly at my side!' Jeanette lives in the Netherlands which she describes as a family oriented country. Children are expected to return home for lunch from school until they are 12. They are therefore taken to and picked up from school four times a day. Jeanette feels that this may be one of the reasons why the employment rate of married women is one of the lowest in Western Europe. Social activities centre around the family and are frequent. Visiting grandparents is a great pastime and if anyone is celebrating a birthday, the housewife is expected to receive relatives and acquaintances all day long. In evenings and at weekends, being together as a family is considered the ideal situation. For a married woman to have a job at all in this climate is quite something, to have a full-time job is unusual. Even women with a minimum of six years university education often prefer to work part-time. If a married woman has the ambition to build a career, it usually becomes a very delicate affair not to distort the picture of a tightly-knit family life too much. This exerts considerable pressure on working women who have to give the impression of 'being around' rather more than in other countries.

If the husband is not around (for whatever reason) the household is allowed to run with much more freedom. Jeanette found that not only did she have greater freedom to concentrate on her work but she was able to make more decisions without consulting her husband. She was able to choose the colours when re-decorating, buy new furniture, rearrange a room or buy the kind of clothes that her husband might not like. She also felt that she was able to deal more consistently with the children in a single parent household.

The separation had its negative side however. Jeanette's husband lived and worked in London while Jeanette and their two sons remained in the Netherlands. Jeanette works as a freelance inter-preter/co-ordinator/consultant bridging Japan and Holland. She was not always at home to take her husband's telephone calls and some-times when he was home on a visit she had other engagements. Jeanette's husband David came home for one weekend every two weeks. Sometimes he would combine these visits with business trips and then the visit would be extended to three or four days. One family vacation was spent in England and Jeanette and the children visited separately on several occasions. David had to run his own house in London and began to view the house in the Netherlands as a kind of paradise – a place to stock up on warmth and care so that he would be equipped to face up to his lonely days in London. David did not enjoy being left out of family decisions but neither did he want to face anything unpleasant during his brief trips home. He 'quietly resented' the fact that Jeanette had found a handyman and had re-designed the garden so that she could handle it herself.

Articles written about commuter marriages talk about the honey-moon feeling which couples are supposed to experience each time they see each other. Jeanette confesses to not knowing what the honeymoon feeling is supposed to be and expressed it like this.

Each time David and I saw each other we needed one or two days of readjustment. David had first to see the changes in the house; I had to mentally decide whether or not I liked his new English clothes, we both had to spit out our good and bad news. During the first couple of days of David's homecoming, the children and I had to get used to explaining our movements to him. David had to accept that we were individuals who kept on changing during his absence. After that came some days of a new appreciation for each other which would not have come had we been living together on a daily basis. That was inevitably followed by a good-bye till next time and 'I love you' at 5.00 a.m. on a Monday morning. Sometimes the transition stage would be so painful that I really wondered whether it was worth-while him coming home less frequently but staying longer. Some women whose husbands returned after several years of separation during a war (and in one case, of illness) also mentioned a difficult period of transition. It took them more than just a few days to readjust then, but on the other hand they did not have the kind of stop go that I had.

Jeanette realised that she counted on fleeting glances to check on David's physical and psychological well-being. They missed the touching and a great deal of non-verbal communication. Jeanette and David used telephoning as their most frequent method of communication, although it had its drawbacks in that finding a good time of day to call on a regular basis was not easy; even a one hour time difference mattered. They finally decided that dinner time was the best and Jeanette recalls 'During that time I ate a lot of cold dinners'.

They also started writing to each other. After a year Jeanette started to keep a journal and send David an instalment every week. She tried to be as honest as if she were writing purely for herself even though that meant David reading some unpleasant things as well as titbits concerning the children and others that she had forgotten to tell him over the 'phone. David said he learned as much about Jeanette through the journal instalments as through all the years of being together. Jeanette feels that the journal saved her sanity and helped David to see what she was going through and that she understood how it was for him.

Jeanette experienced the feelings of desertion which most couples feel when they are separated. The feeling is often accompanied by anger at the partner for having left you. (This same process is also felt during the period immediately after a bereavement or divorce.)

David experienced severe depression manifested in physical symptoms; insomnia, pounding of his heart, stomach ache and continuous fatigue soon after he arrived in London. He was separated from his family, family friends and usual support systems and put in abnormally long hours as compensation. Both the partners had to manage a complex financial situation; the cost of maintaining two households, extra business entertaining for David and income tax which was complicated to work out on a salary that was determined in dollars, paid in pounds with tax paid in gulden. Changes in the exchange rate can affect income by 30–40 per cent and did so negatively for Jeanette and David. Once David re-settled in the Netherlands the period of readjustment was even longer. Generally speaking the readjustment period lasts as long as the period of separation. Jeanette thinks, however, that you will never be the same once you have lived separately for a long time. Every commuter couple agrees that commuting takes up a lot of energy and not only for the one who does the commuting.

When David finally returned to the Netherlands he generated a lot of action to change many things around the house. He bought new furniture, put up some shelves, arranged for a cleaning lady (which they had never had before) and wanted to buy a dog. In spite of the problems Jeanette feels that their relationship has acquired a new dimension. Jeanette has a newly gained sense of freedom and independence to pursue her own career interests which David respects and supports. Through the changes in themselves each has grown closer to, and more appreciative of, the other, but they hope they need never to have to go through it again.

We include this story as a frank example of the very real problems faced by dual career families.

There are similar problems of frustration and anger which are faced by the stay at home wives who take over the running of the home and the management of the children during their husband's absence on shorter business trips. This is frequently expressed as anger by the wife and is taken away by the husband along with the briefcase, the company papers and the suitcase full of clean shirts and pants. The exit and re-entry problems have to be faced several times a year by some families. This can initiate real conflict for the husband who becomes torn between his love for his family and his loyalty to the company. There are occasions when the wife puts forward so much pressure that the husband finally capitulates and settles for a more stable business life, even if it means a change of job and a consequent lowering of income. Either way the company loses. Employees are not performing effectively when they are under stress. This has been so well documented in recent years that we feel we do not need to labour the point. If a company loses a valued employee because of unresolved conflict between work and family they are losing an investment of several thousand pounds which has been put in as training, company knowledge and expertise which a competitor will be pleased to snap up. We would further suggest that the oft-quoted phrase 'if you don't like the heat get out of the kitchen' is a totally unconstructive way of looking at human resource management and spells economic suicide at a time of skill shortages which are already causing problems for many companies.

12 Beyond the Great Divide

It is impossible to sweep away centuries of gender conditioning within just one decade. There are still companies who do not know where to begin. Others have made little effort beyond including a written Equal Opportunities Policy in the staff handbook. The situation at the moment is that a balance of women and men has not been achieved at middle management level and above.

It is unrealistic to expect anyone, whether female or male, to devote 100 per cent of their waking hours to work. If we can accept this we can dispel some of the arguments raised by managers in defence of their refusal to promote women. Women may leave to have babies but men may leave to further their careers. Women are said to lack mobility, so do some men who are reluctant to relocate wife and children if the latter are at a crucial stage in their education and a move would mean the wife giving up her job and a much-needed second income. In dual career families, women and men are now beginning to negotiate over who stays at home if the children get sick. That old, old argument is therefore no longer valid.

Work patterns examined

In spite of the current high rate of unemployment there are still areas where skill shortages are becoming a problem. This is particularly true in the south-east where management and technological skill shortages are acute. Many companies are now making positive attempts to recruit women who wish to return to work after raising a family. Job share schemes and flexible patterns of work are being introduced. The major shift in employment patterns, from heavy construction and industrial work to service and new technology skills, is good news for women who are responding to the challenge. The younger woman is no longer working for pin money but for a real contribution to the family income. Career women are taking shorter career breaks and are generally older when they have their first child. More active consideration is being given to the timing of the career break and more and more women are waiting until they are well established in their career before they begin to raise a family.

Looking to the future company

What then is the future? There is currently much talk of 1992 and the Euro. manager. What needs to be done in order to finally bridge the Great Divide? What skills will be needed by future managers and what action do companies need to take in order to meet the 1992 challenge?

Charles Handy, in his report: 'The Making of Managers', made the following statement:

> Britain needs to do more to develop her managers and to do it more systematically. . . . Business education provides a base for the long-term. The short-term needs more immediate action. . . . One possibility is a Development Code setting out a code of good practice in management development.

At the same time as this report was published, Lord Young was urging Chief Executives in organisations to develop their managers as a central part of their business strategy.

Both these recommendations were taken up by the Council for Management Education and Development under the chairmanship of Bob Reid, Chairman of Shell UK. The Management Charter Initiative was subsequently launched under the aegis of the Confederation of British Industry, the British Institute of Management and the Federation for Management Education. The Management Charter Initiative has the following objectives:

1. The founding of a mass movement of organisations committed to a Code of Practice promoting the development of high standards of modern management practice and business skills at all levels of the economy. (The Management Charter Movement.)
2. The formation of a body, under a Royal Charter, to direct and adminster the Management Charter movement and Chartered management system on a permanent basis, and to advance the practice of professional management and its development.

Today's management will be working in tomorrow's organisation which is already taking shape in those sectors of industry and in the financial services sectors where fierce competition and fluctuation in demand have required companies to become more flexible.

The organisation of tomorrow was outlined by Charles Handy in a series of lectures given to BIM members around the country in 1987. The Shamrock Organisation or the flexible firm will be able to respond readily to peaks and troughs of demand. It will be constructed around a core group of indispensable technically and managerially qualified people who are needed to provide and sell the company's goods or services and to manage those central operations profitably. This core group will be expensive because they are seen as indispensable. They will therefore be the recipients of a good employee package, commensurate with the total commitment which will be demanded of them.

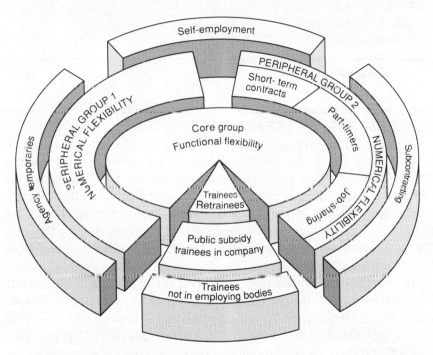

Figure 8 *The flexible firm (Source IMS)*

The core group will be supported by several peripheral groups (see Fig. 8) which will meet a variety of short-term needs. The effectiveness of a company in the future is likely to be judged on a strength-to-weight ratio measured in terms of productivity per permanent employee. The peripheral groups will supply the numerical flexibility which will be required by companies in the future. The peripheral groups can be:

1. Agency temporaries supplying secretarial, cleaning or catering needs.
2. Ex-employees who subcontract their services back to the company when needed. They will, however, be self-employed and free to work for other 'employers' during slack periods.
3. Part-time staff who work as required.
4. Job-sharers – two part-time workers doing what was once a full-time job.
5. External consultants who will provide a variety of professional services including:

> Executive recruitment
> Training and/or management development
> Pay and benefits planning
> Manpower planning
> Market research
> Public relations
> Cleaning services
> Catering services

There will also be some trainees who are subsidised by the Training Commission under the YTS or Employment Training programmes.

The pace of technological change is doubling every seven years, economic change is also rapid and mature industries are becoming a thing of the past. New skills are being demanded by organisations for which the training will need to be advanced and tightly focused. Working hours are rising from 43 hours per week to 47–52 for professional and self-employed people. It is expected that by the year 2000, the working week for manual workers will have dropped from 35–37 hours to 25–28 hours.

The current employment patterns mirror the beginning of the flexible firm. Between 1982 and 1984, 600,000 new jobs were created in the UK. There was a dramatic rise in self-employment with 400,000 of the new jobs being created by individuals. Women took 500,000 of the new jobs and 300,000 men left the labour market during the same period.

The changes in employment patterns for the under 20s have been similarly dramatic. Between 1979 and 1986 the number of teenage part-time workers increased from 116,000 to 407,000, an increase of 250 per cent. The numbers of teenagers in full-time work has fallen from 1.8 million to 1.2 million in the same period. Six out of every ten part-time workers are aged under 20. Nearly 50 per cent of all part-time work is temporary.

Future employment patterns

Some companies offer a flexible year in addition to a flexi-week. The four-day week is a reality with many companies, and has been so for some considerable time. Sabbaticals and secondments are being offered to reduce the pressure on the older executive. The home-based industry of the future will be the 'electronic cottage'. Companies are already becoming flatter with fewer middle managers. New forms of self-employment are categorised as entrepreneurial, buyouts, linked sub-contracting and networking.

Women are moving into self-employment because of the lack of opportunities for promotion in today's organisation; nearly a quarter of all self-employed are women. Industries like direct selling have an almost 90 per cent female workforce, most working as self-employed saleswomen demonstrating their ability to be highly successful businesswomen while catering flexibly for the needs of their families. Direct selling companies are highly supportive in training and enabling women to work independently, they have found it pays dividends to the company just as the large number of 'housewives' earning £15,000 per annum or more have also found it pays. However, there is a feeling that many are becoming self-employed without the necessary experience to run a company profitably.

The senior managers of tomorrow will need a period of overseas work in order to prepare for 1992 and many women are denied this, frequently because the company assumes their lack of mobility. The Institute of Manpower Studies recently carried out a survey of 40 British companies in order to find out the skills they will expect from their managers in the future. Good communication and interpersonal skills are felt to be of paramount importance as are the more usual managerial skills of leadership, judgement, initiative, organisational skills, planning, innovation and decision making. The ability to manage change and stress, and to work as part of a team will be a prerequisite for all managers, scarcely surprising given the accelerated rate of change already indicated.

There is a strong feeling that if women are to secure their long-term position in the workplace, working side-by-side with men as respected colleagues with no pay differential, no development restrictions and no discrimination around promotion; then it is now or never that they must make their presence at work a permanence.

Norman Fowler, Secretary of State for Employment, predicted that 'Britain is on the brink of a revolution in employment opportunities for women that will continue beyond short-term demographic changes.' He went on to add that 'the Government was determined that women should have flexible working conditions' and that 'women have the right to build a career which is every bit as secure, ambitious and satisfying as that of a man'. Mr Fowler was speaking at a conference organised by the Confederation of British Industry and the Equal Opportunities Commission in March 1989 to help focus the business mind on the conflicting demands of home and work. In responding to this statement Joanna Foster, Chair of the EOC, called for government help to turn Mr Fowler's fine words into practical reality. On two occasions during this century women have been pulled from the home and into employment to keep the wheels of industry turning when the men were away fighting in the two world wars. Over 1000 day-nurseries were started during the Second World War and just as rapidly closed when the war was over. Now, when 54 per cent of all women in the UK work, there is still a shortage of child-minders and free nurseries.

It is now that women must show that they are both desirable as employees and indispensable for the skills they bring.

The EEC is planning to introduce positive measures to improve women's rights after 1992. They will be pushing three specific measures:

1. A European Women's lobby to promote equality of rights and opportunities between women and men. It will monitor the implementation of law and policy and draw up new measures to help women at work.
2. A Community prize for business creation for women. The Commission has a scheme to finance the creation by women of local employment initiatives, such as co-operatives and small businesses.
3. A European conference on the effects of 1992 on women's employment.

In putting forward this proposal at the TUC Women's Conference in Blackpool in March 1989 Mrs Vasso Papandreou, the European Commissioner for Social Affairs said:

> There cannot be an 'industrial' Europe, or a 'technological' Community, or a fiscal and monetary union, if there is not at the same time a 'social' Europe. The Community is not some sort of restaurant which allows diners to choose à la carte what they want from the menu, and leave the rest behind.

She was referring to the British veto of the Draft Directive on Parental

Leave. A Community equality programme will contain a significant extension of vocational training to encourage employers to apply equal opportunities and promote positive action for women. An initiative to ease the impact of new technologies on women's employment will run alongside an emphasis on child care. A comparative study on labour law is to be carried out to give the Commission an overview of what exists at national level in every state.

In theory once all the loopholes in current legislation are plugged the woman of tomorrow will be able to progress unimpeded in the post-1992 organisation. Or will she? Looking at the list of Industrial Tribunal cases which have been brought, and successfully fought, during the last decade it would appear that a good deal more than legislation is required to facilitate the advance of women. A major hurdle which must still be overcome is the problem of women and men working together. Looking back to our earlier chapter in which we put forward men's views of women and women's view of men it appears that the first obstacle must be to challenge the assumptions that each sex has of the other. We can then perhaps move forward and begin to assuage the guilt which some of us feel if we deviate from the 'norm' or what for generations has been assumed to be normal behaviour for 'women' and 'men'. In a future organisational world which knows no divide it should be OK for men to be sensitive, caring, listening, enabling and tender and acceptable for women to have career goals in addition to domestic goals, or indeed instead of the more traditional roles. Perhaps this is the time for both sexes to discard the straitjacket which sexuality imposes, 'nice girls don't' and 'big boys do', and to acknowledge that, at work anyway, we are people first committed to helping the environment to change so that for all of us it becomes more comfortable.

We advance this view advisedly because of recent developments which we have noticed, particularly from men, on dual sex courses. It has become apparent to us that not all men are comfortable in today's organisation. Some men are forced into feelings of personal inadequacy because they do not fit the aggressive, macho image which society tells them is 'male'. The word 'wimp' has slipped almost unnoticed into everyday usage and is as derisory for men as virago is for women, conjuring as it does the opposite to what is expected of either sex.

A survey carried out by Apex the white-collar union, and published in March 1989, looked at the difference in attitudes to work of women and men. According to the findings men work for money and career advancement; women on the other hand are looking for job satisfaction, a good working atmosphere and the flexibility to fit family life into their careers. The men in the survey saw little conflict between the demands of home and family and work, and job satisfaction does not appear to be an issue for them, except in the younger 25–40 age group who are highly skilled, well paid, white-collar workers. This group stressed the importance of enjoying the job and expressed concern about the impact of work on their home life. 'I'd like to spend more time at home, but in this job it's all or nothing' one of this group said.

The research suggests, however, that this group are in a minority. Professor Gary Cooper of the Manchester School of Management, University of Manchester, has carried out comparative studies of women and men in 65 different occupations, from oil-rig workers and secretaries to dentists and managers. He has found that no matter what the job is, the same differences between women and men apply. According to Professor Cooper men are always looking up the ladder for the main chance whereas women are looking at doing a thorough job and doing that job well. Professor Cooper explains this difference by saying that because women are relatively new to corporate life they are insecure about their abilities, they therefore concentrate on reaching high standards in each task they are set. Professor Cooper believes that, because of this attitude, women do their jobs better. Men on the other hand are good at playing organisational politics in order to get to the top of the pile but do not necessarily do their jobs well. Men have, in the past, been largely excluded from the domestic arena and the world of work was the only arena in which they could prove themselves.

The conditioning of women, however, has led them to believe that they must look after the whole family and not simply themselves. This has involved them in organising and juggling multiple commitments which makes them better potential managers according to Cooper. It is the attitude of women therefore which is important as a focus for the future. Working for self-fulfilment, for social relationships, to be valued by colleagues and, above all, to have the feeling that she is making a contribution. This leads in turn to less stress at work and less ill health. Although many women are shouldering double burdens, running a home and working, research shows illness rates among women to be lower than those for men. If the men are succumbing to heart attacks and other stress-related illnesses, which they are, and women are living longer, which they are, is this not a powerful argument for a change in attitude?

Changing the culture of an organisation is a difficult process but it must happen if we accept that a workforce composed of two genders is here to stay. Any form of change is likely to meet with resistance which is based on very real individual concerns. It is likely that well-understood work routines will be disrupted, career patterns that could be predicted with some accuracy come under threat in the changing environment, there is suspicion from employees about the motives of top management in seeking to change the culture and fear from the managers themselves that the new culture will not be successful. The most successful organisations in the future will be those that achieve the right balance between the organisational need and those of its work-force. The organisational needs will be concerned with budgets, pro-ductivity and the employees who will help them to achieve their productivity within the stated budget. The employees needs will be for a job which will lead on to a career which is compatible with their desired lifestyle. The culture will enable both sets of objectives to be met. Planning for the future has to begin now, when demographic changes, technological changes and membership of the European Free Market are all major changes which have to be addressed. The planning stage is vital if a supportive environment is to be created to enable employees to grow and flourish side by side. In seeking to cross the Great Divide companies will have to address cultural differences between ourselves and other European countries and to recognise that whether employees are young or old, white or black, female or male, able bodied or disabled and belonging to any layer of society that is preoccupied with class differences, each has a role to play which can ultimately benefit the organisation.

In moving forward there will inevitably be compromises and con-straints but there will also be opportunities and ultimately achievement from which both organisations and employees can benefit. The motiva-tion is the attraction and retention of a high calibre workforce. Almost every week the quality newspapers run an article which addresses the problem of how to recruit the best. Recruitment is an expensive and time-consuming procedure; with annual recruitment costs of £1.5 million and a staff turnover of 137 per cent in London and 103 per cent in the North, one national hotel chain recognises the need for change. A training package 'Caring for People' was chosen to counteract their skills wastage problems with positive results quite simply because by 'people' they included all employees, from kitchen porters to managing director.

Some of the other initiatives which have already been launched have been acknowledged earlier in the book. We have tried to put forward the message that in the organisation of the future there will be no place for staff who are under-utilised, under-valued, under-managed and under-developed. The ideal environment will be planned and facilitated at corporate level and implemented at local level based on an environment of openness, integrity and trust.

There has been a phenomenal amount of activity in the world of work since the introduction of the equal opportunity legislative framework. Women have been writing new scripts for themselves and participating for the first time ever in single-sex training which has helped them to become more assertive, more goal-oriented and has left them with an increasing awareness of self-worth. There has been a tremendous growth in the number of women's networks and ethnic groups which have offered support and encouragement and have followed the example set by men. Men too have been through their single-sex, awareness raising workshops and many are beginning to emerge from the closet and are admitting that they do not much like their current organisation structure. Millions of pounds have been spent on attracting large numbers of women away from domestic responsibilities and back into work. Initiatives have been taken both by organisations and by catalytic individuals who are committed to initiating change.

If we are to cross the Great Divide successfully we have to confront our own, deep-rooted prejudices against those of our colleagues who differ from us in some way either politically, or socially or sexually. We must learn to listen to the people we do not like very much and admit that they have a point to make, an opinion worth hearing. Only then shall we be able to accept that, although our working colleagues are different from us, they each have a unique personality and skills which are special to them but also useful to the organisation. Equal opportunity is not about making everyone the same but rather making use of the differences and finding a plot in which they can successfully grow. A world without divide is one in which we have learned to respect other people and, in return, receive the respect which we as individuals feel we deserve.

Bibliography

Aivaliotis, Marina: *Women's Path to Management in the Hotel and Catering Industry*. Research Report, HCTB, May, 1984.

Bates, M. and D. W. Kiersey: *Please Understand Me*. Prometheus Nemesis Book Company, California, 1984.

Beck, Jane *Managing in a Growth Industry: A Report on an Accelerated Management Development Programme for Women Managers in the Hotel and Catering Industry*. TA, Moorfoot.

Beck, Jane and Sally Beck: A Two-way Mirror, *Women in Management Review*, Vol. 2, No.1.

Bowen, D. D.: Were Men Meant to Mentor Women? *Training and Development Journal*, Feb. 1985.

Bowen., D. D.: 'Identification is to Mentoring as Infatuation is to Love', Paper presented at a meeting of the Academy of Management, Dallas, 1983.

Bowen, D. D. and P. Zollinger: 'Mentoring and the Careers of Women Managers', Paper presented at the meeting of the Academy of Management, Detroit, 1980.

Boydell, Tom and Valerie Hammond: Self Development Groups for Women Managers, *Women & Training News*, Issue 21, Winter, 1985.

Breese, Charlotte and Hilaire Gomer: *The Good Nannie Guide*. Century, Sept. 1988.

Brown, L. K.: *The Woman Manager in the United States*. Business and Professional Women's Federation, Washington 1984.

Clutterbuck, David: *Everyone Needs a Mentor*. Demy, May 1985.

Devine, Marion, (ed.): *Working Together: Developing Effective Partnerships*. EWMD Conference Report. EFMD International Association Centre, Brussels.

Equal Opportunities Commission: *Legislating For Change* HMSO, 1988.

Ferguson, Marilyn: *The Aquarian Conspiracy: Personal and Social Transformation in the 1980's*. Granada, 1982.

Frator, S.: Why Women Aren't Getting to the Top, *Fortune*, 1984.

Garner, Lesley: *How to Survive as a Working Mother*. Jill Norman Ltd, 1980.

Gill, Deidre and Bernard Ungerson: *Equal Pay – The Challenge of Equal Value*.

Harrison, Rosemary, *Training and Development*. Institute of Personnel Management, 1988.

Issues in the Development of Women. Report on Employee Potential – Ashridge Management College and Women in Management Project Team. IPM & TA, 1980.

Job Sharing , Improving the Quality and Availability of Part-time work. EOC, 1981.

Job Sharing: Putting Policy into Practice. New Ways to Work, 309 Upper Street, London N1 2TY.

Kanter, R. M.: *Men and Women of the Corporation.* Basic Books, NY, 1977.

Kinsman, Francis: *The Telecommuters.* Wiley.

Kram, K. E.: 'Mentoring Processes at Work: Developmental Relationships in Managerial Careers'. Unpublished Doctoral Dissertation, Yale University, New Haven.

Lawson, Annette: *Adultery – An Analysis of Love and Betrayal.* Basil Blackwell, Feb. 1989.

Margerison, C. and R. Lewis: Mapping Managerial Styles, *International Journal of Manpower*, Vol. 2, No. 1, 1981.

Mintzberg, H.: *The Nature of Managerial Work.* Harper & Row, New York.

Mintzberg, H.: The Manager's Job: Folklore and Fact, *Harvard Business Review*, July–August, 1975.

Must Part-timers be the Bottom of the Pile, *Personnel Management*, April 1988.

Myers-Briggs, I. *Introduction to Type.* Center for Applications of Psychological Type, Florida, 1976.

No Barriers Here: A Guide to Overcoming Barriers to Women's Career Development. Available from the Training Agency, Moorfoot, Sheffield.

NUPE: *A Fair Deal for Part-Time Workers.* National Union for Public Employees.

Pollert, Anna *The Flexible Firm: A Model in Search of Reality or a Policy in Search of a Practice.* Univ. of Warwick.

Returning to Work: A Directory of Education and Training for Women. Longmans.

Steel, Maggie and Zita Thornton: *Women Can Achieve Career Success* and *Women Can Return to Work.* Thorsons, 1988.

Steinen, G.: *Outrageous Acts and Everyday Rebellions.* Plume, New York 1984.

Taylor, A.: Why Women Managers are Baling Out, *Fortune*, 1986.

Vinnicombe, Susan: What Exactly are the Differences in Male and Female Working Styles? *Women in Management Review*, Vol. 3, No. 1.

Women and Men in Britain: A Research Profile. EOC 1987. HMSO, London.

Woodham-Smith, Cecil: *Florence Nightingale.*

Women, Work and Training: A Manual of Teaching Resources for Use with Men and Women at Work. Training Agency.

Women's Training: A Ten Year Perspective to Mark the UN Decade for Women 1976–1985. Women & Training Group.

Useful addresses

Colleges and Courses for Women

Ashridge School of Management, Little Gaddesdon, Berkhamsted, Herts.
   Tel. 044 284 3491.
Hillcroft College, Southbank, Surbiton, Surrey, KT6 6DF. Tel. 01–399 2688.
Brunel University, Uxbridge, Middlesex, UB8 3PH. Tel. 0895 56461 Ext. 215.
Cranfield School of Management, Cranfield Institute of Technology,
   Cranfield, Beds. Tel. 0234 751122.
Henley – The Management College, Henley on Thames, Oxon, RG9 3AU.
   Tel. 0491 571454.
Roffey Park Management College, Forest Road, Horsham, W. Sussex
   RH12 4TD. Tel. 029 383 644.
The Open University, Open Business School, Walton Hall, Milton Keynes,
   MK7 6AA.
The Open College, PO Box 35, Abingdon, OX14 3BR. Tel. 0235 555444.
Rhownair Centre, Outward Bound Wales, Tywyn, Gwynedd, Wales.
   Tel. 0654 710521.
Outward Bound Trust, Chestnut Field, Regent Place, Rugby, CV21 2PJ.
   Tel. 0788 60423.

UK Resources/departing expatriates

Focus Information Service, 47–49 Gower Street, London WC1E 6HR.
   Tel. 01–631 4367.
FOCUS members, comprising over fifteen nationalities have listed the cities
in which they have lived. Currently there are 32 US cities and 48 cities
outside the US represented. The members are willing to speak with
prospective residents of the cities in which they have lived. FOCUS has also
contact organisation names and addresses in other cities and as a member of
Catalyst in New York, listings of resource centres throughout the 50 states.

Women's Corona Society, Minister House, 274 Vauxhall Bridge Road,
London SW1V 1BB. Tel. 01–828 1652/3.
The Society's primary aim is to provide information, advice and personal
contacts for people going abroad in whatever capacity. It offers a *Notes for*

Newcomers booklet series and 'Living Overseas', one-day courses, six times a year.

The Centre for International Briefing, The Castle, Farnham, Surrey, GU9 0AG. Tel. 0252–721194.
The Centre was established to help people to adapt quickly and imaginatively to the changes they would experience when taking up residence or travelling on business overseas. Many courses are offered and an extensive library is available.

Embassies and High Commissions, The Commonwealth Institute, Kensington High Street, London W8. Tel. 01–603 4535.
Commonwealth Countries League, 99 The Grove, Isleworth, Mddx. TW7 4JE. Tel. 01–560 8142.

Agencies offering courses for women

The Pepperell Unit, The Industrial Society, 3 Carlton House Terrace, London W1. Tel. 01–839 4300.
Monadnock, The Chapel, RVPB, Fitzhugh Grove, London SW18 1SX. Tel. 01–871 2546.
Domino Training Ltd, 56 Charnwood Road, Shepshed, Leics. LE12 9NP. Tel. 0509–505404.
Myrtle Berman, 2 Hillside, Highgate Road, London NW5 1QT. Tel. 01–485 7482.
The Rennie Fritchie Consultancy, Suite 6, The Business Centre, Innsworth Technology Park, Innsworth Lane, Gloucester GL3 1DL. Tel. 0452–731499.
Beck Associates, 185 Lord Street, Hoddesdon, Herts, EN11 8NQ. Tel. 0992–464966.
Women CAN, 32 The Mall, Southgate, London N14 6LN. Tel. 01–886 5848.
Entek, The Mansion, Minchenden, High Street, London N14 6BJ. Tel. 01–886 0057.

Training Agency Offices

London Region

London North, 6th Floor, 19–29 Woburn Place, London WC1 0LU. Tel. 01–837 1288.
London North East, 3rd Floor, Cityside House, 40 Adler Street, London E1 1EW. Tel. 01–377 1866.
London South and West, Lyric House, 149 Hammersmith Road, Hammersmith, London W14 0QL. Tel. 01–602 7227.

London South East, Skyline House, 200 Union Street, London SE1 0LX.
Tel. 01–928 0800.

Midlands Region

Birmingham and Solihull, 15th and 16th Floors, Metropolitan House, 1
Hagley Road, Birmingham, B16 8TG. Tel. 021–454 3355.
Coventry and Warwickshire, 5th and 6th Floors, Bankfield House. 163 New
Union Street, Coventry, CV1 2PE. Tel. 0203–24100.
Derbyshire, 4th Floor, St. Peter's House, Gower Street, Derby, DE1 1SB.
Tel. 0332–360550.
Dudley and Sandwell, Falcon House, The Minories, Dudley, DY2 8PG.
Tel. 0384–238391.
Leicestershire and Northamptonshire, 1st Floor, Rutland Centre, Halford
Street, Leicester, LE1 1TQ. Tel. 0533–538616.
Lincolnshire, Wigford House, Brayford Wharf, Lincoln, LN5 7AY.
Tel. 0522–32266.
Nottinghamshire, 4th Floor, Lambert House, Talbot Street, Nottingham, NG1
7FF. Tel. 0602–413313.
Shropshire, Hereford and Worcestershire, Hazledene House, Town Centre,
Telford, Shropshire, TF3 4JJ. Tel. 0952 507474.
Staffordshire, Moorlands House, 24 Trinity Street, Hanley, Stoke-on-Trent,
ST1 5LN. Tel. 0782–260505.
Wolverhampton and Walsall, 2nd Floor, Burdett House, 29–30 Cleveland
Street, Wolverhampton, WV1 3HA. Tel. 0902 711111.

Northern region

Cleveland, Corporation House, 73 Albert Road, Middlesbrough, Cleveland,
TS1 2RU. Tel. 0642–241144.
Co. Durham, Valley Street North, Darlington, Co. Durham, DL1 1TJ.
Tel. 0325–51166.
Northumberland, North Tyneside and Newcastle, 1st Floor, Broadacre
House, Market Street, Newcastle upon Tyne, NE1 6HH. Tel. 0632–326181.
Sunderland, South Tyneside and Gateshead, Derwent House, Washington
New Town, Tyne and Wear, NE38 7ST. Tel. 091–416 6161.

North-West region

Bolton, Bury, Rochdale and Wigan, 3rd Floor, Provincial House, Nelson
Square, Bolton, BL1 1PN. Tel. 0204–397350.
Cheshire, 1st Floor, Spencer House, Dewhurst Road, Birchwood Centre,
Warrington, WA3 7PP. Tel. 0925–826515.
Cumbria, 1st and 2nd Floors, Thirlmere Block, Mobet Estate, Workington,
Cumbria, CA14 3YB. Tel. 0900–66991.

Lancashire, 2nd, 3rd and 4th Floors, Duchy House, 96 Lancaster Road, Preston, PR1 1HE. Tel. 0772–59393.

Liverpool Inner, 4th Floor, Sefton House, Exchange Street East, Liverpool, L2 3XR. Tel. 051–236 0026.

Liverpool Outer, 7th Floor, Sefton House, Exchange Street East, Liverpool, L2 3XR. Tel. 051–236 0026.

Manchester, Salford and Trafford, 4th and 5th Floors, Boulton House, 17–21 Chorlton Street, Manchester M1 3HY. Tel. 061–236 7222.

Oldham, Tameside and Stockport, 1st Floor, 1 St Peter's Square, Stockport, SK1 1NN. Tel. 061–477 8830.

Scotland

Ayrshire, Dumfries and Galloway, 25 Bank Street, Kilmarnock, KA1 1ER. Tel. 0563–44044.

Central and Fife, 5 Kirk Loan, Corstophine, Edinburgh, EH12 7HD. Tel. 031–334 9821.

Dumbarton, Argyll and Renfrewshire, 5 Elm Bank Gardens, Charing Cross, Glasgow, G2 4PN. Tel. 041–226 5544.

Glasgow City, George House, 4th Floor, 36 North Hanover Street, Glasgow, G1 2AD. Tel. 041–552 3411.

Grampian and Tayside, 4th and 5th Floors, Argyll House, Marketgait, Dundee, DD1 1UD. Tel. 0382–29971.

Highlands and Islands, 3rd Floor, Metropolitan House, 31–33 High Street, Inverness, IV1 1TX. Tel. 0463–220555.

Lanarkshire, Scomagg House, Crosshill Street, Motherwell, ML1 1RU. Tel. 0698– 51411.

Lothian and Borders, 2–3 Queen Street, Edinburgh, EH2 1JS. Tel. 031–225 1377.

South-East region

Bedfordshire and Cambridgeshire, 6th and 7th Floors, King House, George Street West, Luton, LU1 2DD. Tel. 0582–412828.

Berkshire and Oxfordshire, 8th Floor, Reading Bridge House, Reading Bridge Road, Reading, Berks, RG1 8PY. Tel. 0734–586262.

Buckinghamshire and Hertfordshire, 2nd Floor, 31 Octagon Parade, High Wycombe, Bucks, HP11 2LD. Tel. 0494–33473.

Essex, Globe House, New Street, Chelmsford, Essex, CM1 1UG. Tel. 0245–358548.

Hampshire and Isle of Wight, 25 Thackeray Mall, Fareham Shopping Centre, Fareham, Hants, PO16 0PQ. Tel. 0329 285921.

Kent, 6th Floor, Victory House, Meeting House Lane, Chatham, Kent, ME4 3PS. Tel. 0634–44411.

Norfolk and Suffolk, Crown House, Crown Street, Ipswich, Suffolk, IP1 3HS.
  Tel. 0473–218951.
Surrey, East and West Sussex, Exchange House, Worthing Road, Horsham,
  West Sussex, RH12 1SQ. Tel. 0403–50244.

South-West region

Avon, PO Box 164, 4th Floor, Minster House, 27 Baldwin Street, Bristol,
  BS99 7HR. Tel. 0272–277116.
Devon and Cornwall, 6th Floor, Intercity House, Plymouth Station,
  Plymouth, Devon, PL4 6AA. Tel. 0752–671671.
Dorset and Somerset, Ground Floor, Michael Paul House, Corporation
  Street, Taunton, Somerset, TA1 4BE. Tel. 0823–85177.
Gloucestershire and Wiltshire, 33–35 Worcester Street, Gloucester GL1 3AJ.
  Tel. 0452–24488.

Wales

Dyfed and West Glamorgan, 3rd Floor, Orchard House, Orchard Street,
  Swansea, SA1 5AP. Tel. 0792–460355.
Gwent, Government Building, Cardiff Road, Newport, Gwent, NP9 1YE.
  Tel. 0633–56161.
Gwynedd, Clwyd and Powys, Wynnstay Block, Hightown Barracks, Kingsmill
  Road, Wrexham, LL13 8BH. Tel. 0978 365550.
Mid and South Glamorgan, 5th Floor, Phase One Building, Ty Glas Road,
  Llanishen, Cardiff, CF4 5PJ. Tel. 0222–755744.

Yorkshire and Humberside Region

Wakefield, Doncaster and Barnsley, York House, 31–16 York Place, Leeds,
  LS1 2EB. Tel. 0532–450502.
Bradford, Calderdale and Kirklees, Jubilee House, 33–41 Park Place, Leeds,
  LS1 2RL. Tel. 0532–446299.
Humberside, 4th Floor, Essex House, Manor Street, Hull, HU1 1YA.
  Tel. 0482–226491.
North Yorkshire and Leeds, Fairfax House, Merrion Street, Leeds, LS2 8LH.
  Tel. 0532 446181.
Sheffield and Rotherham, 8th Floor, Sheaf House, The Pennine Centre,
  Hawley Street, Sheffield, S1 3GA. Tel. 0742–701911.

Women's Groups list

An alphabetical listing of some of the women's networking groups in the UK
and Europe. The list has been compiled through the readership of *Women &*

Training News the quarterly Newsletter of the 'Women & Training Group'.
The list comprises professional, company-based and multidisciplinary
networks all of whom are dedicated to helping women at work.

300 Group, 9 Poland Street, London W1V 3DG. Tel. 01–734 3457.

Association of British Dental Surgery Assistants, DSA House, 29 London
  Street, Fleetwood, Lancashire, FY7 6JY. Tel. 039–17 78631.

Association of Women Travel Executives, Editor, Ms A. Chessel,
  Travelwoman, c/o Austrian Airlines, 50 Conduit Street, London W1R 0NP.
  Tel. 01–439 1851.

Academic Women's Achievement Group, Professor Hannah Steinberg,
  University College London, Gower Street, London WC1 6BT.
  Tel. 01– 387 7050 Ext. 7232.

Association of Women Solicitors, Membership Secretary Miss P. R.
  Cunningham, Ipsley Court, Berrington Close, Upsley, Redditch,
  Worcestershire, B98 0TD. Tel. 0527–517141.

Association of Women in Public Relations, President Tina Hancock, c/o
  Condor Public Relations, 299 Oxford Street, London W1R 1LA. Tel.
  01–499 7324.

British Association of Women Entrepreneurs, Nora Liddle Terek, 303 Preston
  Road, Harrow, Mddx. Tel. 01–904 1412.

British Federation of University Women, Crosby Hall, Cheyne Walk, London
  SW3 5BA. Tel. 01–352 5354.

British Women Pilots' Association, Hon. Secretary, Barbara Kiell, Rochester
  Airport, Chatham, Kent, ME5 9SD. Tel. 0634–816340.

British Women's Travel Club Limited, Trisha Cochrane, 10 Strutton Ground,
  London SW1P 2HP. Tel. 01–222 4539.

Centre for Research on European Women, 38 Rue Stevin, 1040 Brussels,
  Belgium. Tel. 02 230 4777.

City Women's Network, Administrative Office, 925 Uxbridge Road,
  Hillingdon Heath, Mddx. UB10 0NJ. Tel. 01–569 2351.

Commonwealth Secretariat Women & Development Programme,
  Marlborough House, Pall Mall, London, SW1Y 5HX. Tel. 01–839 3411.

Cornwall Women's Network, c/o Frances Chiell, Cornwall College, Pool,
  Redruth, Cornwall, TR15 3RD. Tel. 0209–712911.

European Union of Women, Executive Secretary Mrs M. A. Backes JP, 32
  Smith Square, London, SW1P 3HH. Tel. 01–222 9000.

European Women's Management Development Network (EWMD), Rue
  Washington 40, B– 1050 Brussels, Belgium. Tel. 02 648 03 85.

European Women's Management Development Network (EWMD), Geraldine
  Brown, Domino Training Limited, 56 Charnwood Road, Shepsted,
  Leicestershire, LE12 9NP. Tel. 0509–505404.

Executive Secretaries Club, President June P S Tatum, 34 Chestnut Avenue,
  Gosfield, Near Halstead, Essex, CO9 1TD. Tel. 0787 472649.

Fawcett Society, 46 Harleyford Road, London SE11 5AY. Tel. 01–587 1287.

Gender & Mathematics Association, c/o Lesley Jones, Faculty of Education, Goldsmiths College, University of London, New Cross, London SE14 6NW. Tel. 01–692 7171, Ext. 2265.

Institute of Qualified Private Secretaries, Miss R. Betts, 126 Farnham Road, Slough, SL1 4XA. Tel. 0753–22395.

London Women & Manual Trades, 52–54 Featherstone Street, London EC1Y 8RT. Tel. 01–251 9192.

Medical Women's Federation, Executive Secretary Mrs V. Lention, Tavistock House North, Tavistock Square, London WC1H 9HX. Tel. 01–387 7765.

Microsystem, Wesley House, 4 Wild Court, Off Kingsway, London WC2B 5AU. Tel. 01–430 0655.

National Advisory Centre of Careers for Women, Secretary Mrs. J. Hurley, Artillery House, Artillery Row, London SW1P 1RT. Tel. 01–799 2129.

National Association of Women Pharmacists, Mrs P. Baker, 40 Norwood, Thornhill, Cardiff, CF4 9DE. Tel. 0222–755638/492832.

National Council of Women GB, 36 Danbury Street, Islington, London N1 8JU. Tel. 01–354 2395.

National Organisation for Women's Management Education (NOWME) Administrator, Grove Cottage, New Barn Lane, Westerham, Kent, TN16 2HT. Tel. 0959 74290.

Network, Irene Harris, Suite 12, Second Floor, The Chambers, Chelsea Harbour, London SW10 OXF. Tel. 01–376 4799.

North West Gas Women's Networking Group, District Administrative Officer, Sheila Hesketh, British Gas, North Western, Gould Street, Manchester M4 4DJ. Tel. 061 832 3030, Ext. 6480.

Scottish Convention of Women, The Secretary, c/o YWCA, 7 Randolph Crescent, Edinburgh, EH3 7TH

Scottish Joint Action Group, Chairwoman Grace Franklin, Seacroft, 13 Titchfield Road, Troon, Ayrshire, KA10 6AN. Tel. 0292–314228.

The Media Committee of the Fawcett Society, 46 Harleyford Road, London SE11 5AY. Tel. 01–587 1287.

Soroptimist International of Great Britain and Ireland, 63 Bayswater Road, London W2 3PJ. Tel. 01–262 4794.

Trade Union Congress (Women's Committee & ER Dept) Secretary Ms Kay Carberry, Congress House, 23–28 Great Russell Street, London WC1B 3LS. Tel. 01–636 4030.

UK Federation of Business and Professional Women, 23 Andsell Street, London W8 5BN. Tel. 01–938 1729.

Women & Training Essex, Joy MacMillan, Chelmsford College of FE, Dovedale, Moulsham Street, Chelmsford, Essex, CM2 OJQ. Tel. 0245–265611.

Women & Training Humberside, Maureen Foers, Northern Business School, Conservancy Buildings, Whitefriargate, Hull, HU1 2EE. Tel. 0482–25562.

Women & Training London, Maureen Scholefield/Sue Mochrie Cullen,
Scholefield Associates, 15 Harwood Road, Fulham, London SW6 4QP.
Tel. 01–736 6975.

Women & Training North East, Helen Wilkinson/Christine Atkinson,
Pentagon Troy Limited, Vermont House, Concord, Washington 11 NE37
2SQ. Tel. 091–389 1014.

Women & Training South East, Jane Beck, Beck Associates, 185 Lord Street,
Hoddesdon, Herts, EN11 8NQ. Tel. 0992–464966.

Women & Training Yorkshire, Carole Truman, School of Social Analysis,
University of Bradford, Richmond Road, Bradford, BD7 1DP. Tel.
0274–733466.

Women & Training Norfolk/Suffolk, Diane DeBell/Liz Bargh, Glebe House,
Stockshill, Bawburgh, Norwich, NR9 3LL. Tel. 0603–811600.

Women & Training Oxford/Swindon/Reading, Bridget Farrands, Walnut
House, High Street, Standford-in-the-Vale, Swindon, SN7 8NQ. Tel. 03677
699.

Women & Training South West, Claire Sheldon/Anne-Marie Saunders,
Ecclesiastical Ins. Office plc, Beaufort House, Brunswick Road, Gloucester,
GL1 1JZ. Tel. 0452–28533.

Women & Work Programme, Coventry Polytechnic, 61 Corporation Street,
Coventry, CV1 19Q. Tel. 0203–227273.

Women Returners' Network, WRN Secretary Ann Bell, Principal, Chelmsford
AEC, Patching Hall Lane, Chelmsford, Essex, CM1 4DB. Tel. 0245.
358631.

Women in Construction, Advisory Group, Room 182, Southbank House,
Black Prince Road, London SE1 7SJ. Tel. 01–587 1802/1507.

Women in Banking, Fay Simcock, Peat Marwick McLintock Management
Consultants, PO Box 486, 1 Puddledock, Blackfriars, London EC4V 3PD.
Tel. 01–236 8000, Ext. 6576.

Women in Enterprise, 26 Bond Street, Wakefield, WF1 2QP. Tel.
0924–361789.

Women in Fundraising Development, Chair Membership Committee Sally
Jones, 17 Sahckstead Lane, Goldalming, Surrey, GU7 1RL.

Women in Housing, c/o HERA, 8th Floor, Artillery House, Artillery Row,
London SW1. Tel. 01 799 2128.

Women in Libraries, London Women's Centre, Wesley House, 4 Wild Court,
London WC2B 5AU.

Women in Management, Executive Secretary Elizabeth Harman, 64 Marryat
Road, Wimbledon, London SW19 5BN. Tel. 01–946 1238.

Women in Medicine, 15 Lyons Fold, Sale, Cheshire, M33 1LF.
Tel. 061–973 7160.

Women in Property, 58 Bloomsbury Street, London WC1B 3QT.
Tel. 01–255 3396.

Women into Business, Irene Jeffrey, 32 Smith Square, London SW1P 3HH.
Tel. 01–222 0330.

Women's Advertising Club of London, Honorary Secretary Ros Todd, Donavon Data Systems, 7 Farm Street, London W1X 7RB. Tel. 01–629 7654.

Women's Computer Centre, Wesley House, 4 Wild Court, London WC2B 5AU. Tel. 01–430 0112.

Women's Engineering Society, Imperial College of Science and Technology, Department of Civil Engineering, Imperial College Road, London SW7 2BU. Tel. 01–589 5111, Ext. 4731.

Women's Enterprise Development Agency, Elaine Lawrence, Aston Science Park, Love Lane, Aston Triangle, Birmingham, B7 4BJ. Tel. 021–359 0178.

Women's Film Television and Video Network, 79 Wardour Street, London W1V 3PH. Tel. 01 434 2076.

Women's National Commission, Government Offices, Horse Guards Road, London SW1P 3AL. Tel. 01–270 5903 (answerphone).

Women's Motor Mechanics Workshop Limited, Bay 4R, 1–3 Brixton Road, London SW9 6DE. Tel. 01–582 2574.

Zonta International, Area Director UK Sheila Marshall, 20 Upland Park Road, Oxford, OX2 7RU. Tel. 0865–59636.

Women's Training Network, c/o East Leeds Women's Workshops, 161 Harehills Lane, Leeds, LS8 3QE. Tel. 0532–499031.

Further information on these groups is published in *Women & Training News* available free of charge from Fiona Price, 'Women & Training Group' Hewmar House, 120 London Road, Gloucester, GL1 3PL. Tel. 0452–309330.

Index